GREAT AMERICAN FAMILIES

GREAT AMERICAN FAMILIES

WITHDRAWN

Gore Vidal V. S. Pritchett David Caute
Bruce Chatwin Peter Conrad
Edward Jay Epstein

W · W · NORTON & COMPANY · INC ·

NEW YORK

First published in America in 1977 by W. W. Norton & Company Inc., New York

Designed by Gilvrie Misstear

First published (in part) in The Sunday Times Magazine, London
Texts © Gore Vidal, V. S. Pritchett, Peter Conrad, Edward Jay Epstein, Bruce Chatwin, David Caute
© Times Newspapers Ltd., London, 1975
ISBN 0-393-98752-2
Printed and bound in Japan by Dai Nippon Printing Co., (Hong Kong) Ltd.

CONTENTS

Introduction by Gore Vidal

The Inventors of the United States decided that there would be no hereditary titles in God's country. Although the Inventors were hostile to the idea of democracy and believed profoundly in the sacredness of property and the necessary dignity of those who owned it, they did not like the idea of king, duke, marquess, earl. Such a system of hereditary nobility was liable to produce aristocrats who tended to mix in politics (like the egregious Lord North) instead of politically responsible burghers.

But the Inventors were practical men and the Federal constitution that they assembled in 1787 was an exquisite machine that, with a repair here and a twist there, has gone on protecting the property of the worthy for 200 years whilst protecting in the Bill of Rights (that sublime after-thought) certain freedoms of speech and assembly which are still unknown even now to that irritable fount of America's political and actual being, old Europe. The Inventors understood human greed and self interest. Combining brutal cynicism with a Puritan sense of virtue, they used those essential drives to power the machinery of the state. If Karl Marx had taken seriously the debates of the Inventors as set forth in the Federalist papers, his vision of the good society might have been

less pure but the harvests in the vast Ukraine might today equal those of smaller Iowa.

From the beginning, greed and vanity and envy were accepted by the Inventors as being the human norm and no-one thought to change the way people were. In 1796, conservative inventor John Jay wrote:

"As to political reformation in Europe or elsewhere, I confess that . . I do not amuse myself with dreams about an age of reason. I am content that little men should be as free as big ones and have and enjoy the same rights, but nothing strikes me as more absurd than projects to stretch little men into big ones, or shrink big men into little ones . . . We must take men and measures as they are, and act accordingly."

That is the very voice of the American Inventors: conservative, common-sensical and just – within (as opposed to the age of) reason.

The problem of a republic is even more profound than that of a democracy (since the latter usually ends up being guided by a dictatorship-of-all-the-people or some such phrase to disguise our old friend oligarchy). A republic is managed not so much by an oligarchy as it is by an establishment, and there is a world of difference between the two categories. The Inventors

hoped that by *not* having an hereditary nobility, they would avoid the British system of dilettante-peers mucking about in a political world they did not understand because peers tended to be landed (i.e. feudal) and the 18th-century world was already one of trade and manufactures, activities that hereditary peers do not understand since they do not trade or make things.

At the Constitutional Convention in Philadelphia a few romantics fought a losing battle to make Washington king and to create a peerage using the odd title 'margrave'. The matter was then settled, the Inventors thought, once and for all. Government would be by the best people in order to forward the best interests of the country's owners. They might have invented the word 'meritocracy' had they not had the same prejudice against neologisms that they had against new men.

But wherever the Lord raises a temple, there the devil puts a brothel. Our 'best' people might not have titles but they do have names; they also acquire fortunes which they pass on to sons and to grandsons and to great-grandsons. As a result, the history of the American republic is the history of certain families, of names that are now every bit as awesome as titles. Swift and Armour . . . one sees a million, a billion little pigs and fat heifers transforming themselves before our eyes into hot dogs and hamburgers and heart attacks for those who eat them. Rockefeller, Firestone, Ford, Chrysler . . . these are imperial names known to all the world, and those who bear them move like viceroys among the common people whose lives are dominated by those great magnates who manufacture, service and repair automobiles. Dupont, Kellogg, Hershey, Woolworth . . . drugs, food, shops: the power and glory of such names are world-wide.

Politically, there are American dynasties far older than, say, the Asquith-Bonham-Carter connection. Saltonstalls and Byrds have been politically active almost as long as the Cecils (and to about as much good end). Yet by some curious turn of fate the principal Inventors did not have proper male heirs . . . no Washington, Jefferson, Madison, Franklin has been heard from since the morning of the nation. Later political families continue to exert a certain mystique. The Roosevelts entered public life in the middle of the last century, producing two presidents; while the Kennedy family only goes back to *Madame Mère's* father, a mayor of Boston. But the Kennedys are instant-dynasty, the creation of those television techniques which diminish even as they exalt. 7

ADAMS

Gore Vidal

Opposite: John Adams, second President of the United States. A plaster life mask made in 1825, the year before he died.
Overleaf: *The Declaration of Independence* (detail), painted by John Trumbull.
Prominent among the signatories was John Adams (standing on the left of the central group).

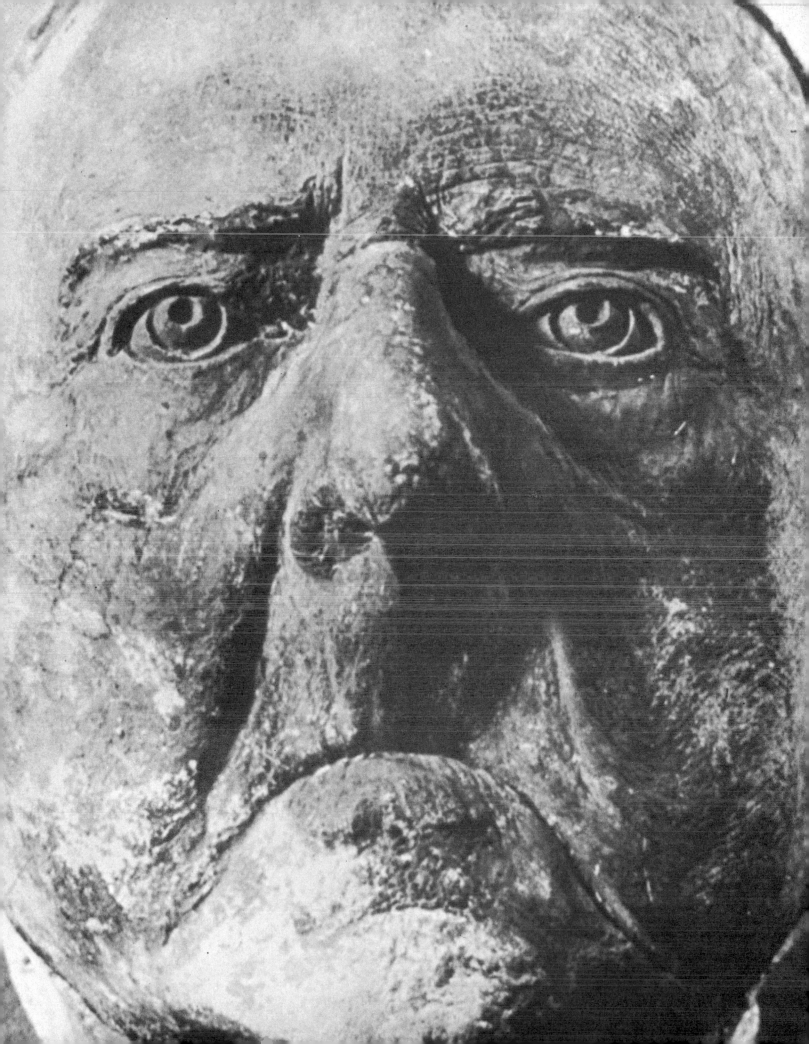

First among the country's political families are the Adamses. In four successive generations the Adams family produced not only two presidents but a number of startlingly brilliant men and women, culminating in the country's only major historian Henry Adams, the bright light of the Fourth (and last splendid) Generation that ended with the death of Henry's brother Brooks Adams in 1927.

To try to understand the Adamses one must begin by placing them. The first Adams to come to America was a copyhold farmer in Somerset, on land belonging to the Lord of the Manor of Barton St David. For reasons unknown, this Henry Adams, with wife and nine children, emigrated to Boston in 1636. Possible sign of character? Of proto-Puritanism? Most English emigrants of that period preferred the balmy West Indies to the cold arduousness of New England.

Ten years later, Adams died, leaving a comfortable property. The next three generations produced dim but increasingly prosperous farmers. In the fourth generation, farmer-militia officer-church deacon John Adams performed that obligatory act of all families destined to distinguish themselves. He committed hypergamy by marrying Susanna Boylston of Brookline, Massachusetts. The Boylstons were distinguished physicians and for an Adams to consort with a Boylston was very much a step up in that little world. Their first child was John Adams (born October 19, 1735); and with him the family entered history, remaining at the centre of national and sometimes world affairs for nearly two centuries.

John Adams was a small plump man, fierce of face and brusque of manner and very much unlike everyone else. Although he was a true child of the bleak New England countryside (and mind), he was a good deal more complicated than any of the other Inventors, saving Jefferson. Adams kept, intermittently, a diary; he composed some chaotic fragments of autobiography; and he copied out most of his letters. Adams thought a very great deal about himself (and of himself), and much of his worrying is now available in the many yards of microfilm devoted to his papers.

At the age of 44, John Adams scrutinised his own character: "There is a Feebleness and a Languor in my Nature. My Mind and Body both partake of this Weakness." Like so many valetudinarians, John Adams suffered good health until the age of 91. "By my Physical Constitution I am but an ordinary Man. The Times have destined me to Fame – and even these have not been able to give me much." Note the irritability; the sense that fate – or something – does not properly value him. This will be one of the family's important recurring motifs. "Yet some great Events, some cutting Expressions, some mean Hypocricies, have at Times, thrown this Assemblage of Sloth, Sleep, and littleness into Rage a little like a Lion."

John Adams could not be better described. He was indeed born at the right time and in the right place and at great moments he was more than a little like a lion. But he was also a Puritan. He worried about his vanity. When his legal career started to flourish, he wrote, "What is the end and purpose of my studies, journeys, labours . . . ? Am I grasping at money or scheming for power? Am I planning the illustration of my family or the welfare of my country? These are great questions . . . Which of these lies nearest my heart?"

The answer of course is that all these things can dwell in reasonable harmony within the same great bosom. But only a New England Puritan would fret so. Certainly one does not find in Franklin, Jefferson or Washington any of the cold-eyed self-scrutiny that the first and all the subsequent Adamses turned upon themselves. Happily, the Adamses were not uncritical of others. In fact, a certain censoriousness is very much the family style. John Adams managed to quarrel hugely with Franklin, Jefferson and, disastrously, with the co-leader of his own party Alexander Hamilton. He also did not much like the cold self-loving and self-satisfied grandeur of his predecessor in the office of first magistrate, George Washington.

The facts of John Adams's early career are unremarkable. He attended Harvard; studied law; was admitted to the bar in 1758 at Boston. Had the English Ministry not managed so entirely to outrage its American colonies, John Adams would be known today, if at all, as a sharp New England lawyer who kept a diary not so good as Pepys. As it was, by the age of 36, he had the largest law practice in the colony. He owned a house at Braintree near Boston and he commuted between country and town as much as he commuted between the private practice of law and public life. "Farewell politics," he writes time and again. But with the American Revolution it was farewell to private life for 30 years.

"The year 1765 has been the most remarkable Year of my Life. That enormous Engine, fabricated by the British Parliament, for battering down all the Rights and Liberties of America, I mean the Stamp Act, has raised and spread, thro the whole Continent a Spirit that will be recorded to our Honour, with all future Generations."

Adams was one of those chosen to present the objections of the people of Massachusetts to the taxes levied on them by the faraway Ministry at London. When selected by his fellow citizens, Adams wondered how it was that someone "unknown as I am" should

Abigail Adams – wife of John, mother of John Quincy

John Adams, up-and-coming barrister, painted in 1766

have been thrust into history. Obviously some "secret invisible Laws of Nature" were at work. This is to be one of the family's principal themes, ultimately expressed in Henry Adams's theory of history.

But no matter how or why John Adams was chosen by the *Zeitgeist* to lead, he more than any other Inventor prepared the way intellectually and rhetorically for the Revolution (as Americans like to call the slow separation of the colonies from England). "I grounded my Argument on the Invalidity of the Stamp Act, it not being in any sense our Act, having never consented to it." Or, "No taxation without representation". With that mighty line, the United States were born as a political entity and in the two hundred years since that noble genesis the government of those states has blithely taxed other peoples (the Filipinos, the residents of the District of Columbia) without for a moment allowing *them* representation.

Adams was a member of the Continental Congress from 1774–78. By seconding the nomination of the Virginian George Washington as commander-in-chief, he insured Washington's selection. Alas. From that moment on Adams regarded Washington rather the way Baron Frankenstein was to regard *his* handiwork. At 40, Adams toyed with the idea of winning glory as a soldier; but decided that he was "too old, and

too much worn with fatigues of study in my youth". Yet he was three years younger than Washington; but then Washington had never fatigued himself with books.

In November 1777 Adams was bored with the Congress and heartily sick of the great Washington. But Congress was not bored with Adams. He was sent in February 1778 to France, to join the other American representatives there, chief among them Benjamin Franklin. Adams admitted that Franklin was "a great genius, a great wit, a great humorist, a great satirist, and a great politician". After all, Adams happened to be none of those things and did not value them. But he did doubt if Franklin was "a great philosopher, a great moralist, and a great statesman . . ." like John Adams.

Adams took with him to Europe his 10-year-old son John Quincy, a future diplomat and president. The education of John Quincy Adams was to be the most superb of any of the American presidents, and consequently absolutely crippling: he was too brilliant and too addicted to toil; he knew too many languages, books, nations, political and philosophical systems to be able to preside with any grace or tolerance over the dingy republic of his day. But in late 18th-century Europe the boy was wide-eyed and impressionable. 13

The second generation: President John Quincy Adams, son of John, and his wife Louisa, a Maryland beauty who disliked New England society. Right: the family house in Quincy, Massachusetts.

14

16 **Charles Francis Adams, son of John Quincy, and his wife, the rich and formidable Abigail Brooks. He died in 1886, thr**

rs after this photograph was taken.

The world was his.

In due course, John Adams was chosen to negotiate the peace with England. After seven dreadful years Washington had finally blundered not into a clear-cut American victory over the English but into a situation where a nervous and weary Ministry at London wanted finally to cut its losses in America. Summarily, the English abandoned their former colonies and went home.

For three successive generations each head of the Adams family was, in a sense, made by England, for each was American minister at London during a crisis and each did his job satisfactorily, if sometimes tactlessly. Or as Sir John Temple noted of John Adams, "he is the most ungracious man I ever saw."

Negotiations with the English themselves were not as difficult for Adams as getting on with his two American co-negotiators Franklin and Jay: "the one malicious, the other, I think honest . . . Franklin's cunning will be to divide us; to this end he will provoke, he will insinuate, he will intrigue, he will manoeuvre." As it turned out, Franklin was not all that bad and Jay was brilliant. Meanwhile, the 14-year-old John Quincy Adams left the school he was attending at The Hague and went off to be secretary to the American minister at St Petersburg. The education was proceeding uniquely well. John Quincy now spoke French, Dutch, German; knew Latin and Greek.

In 1785 John Adams was appointed first American minister to England, and set up shop at a house in Grosvenor Square (£160 per annum). Everyone came to call, even Lord North. By then Adams had been joined by his wife Abigail. In marrying the daughter of the noted Reverend William Smith and the very grand Elizabeth Quincy, Adams had, like his father, committed the obligatory act of hypergamy: his children were now related to *everyone* in Massachusetts.

The sharp-tongued Abigail was a devoted wife and a fine letter writer. Although her eldest son John Quincy Adams was, from the beginning, a paragon, the second son Charles took to drink and died at 30 while a daughter married not too well. But Abigail's principal interest was not her children but her prickly husband and their marriage was happy. Certainly they had a fine time in England, despite Adam's occasional fits of republican censoriousness. After visiting Stowe, Blenheim, Wotton, Osterley, as well as "Ld. Littleton's seat" where he was impressed by "the Grandness and Beauty of the Scenes", Adams felt obliged to add, "It will be long, I hope before Ridings, Parks, Pleasure Grounds, Gardens and ornamented Farms grow so much in fashion in America." Happily, Adams never

An Adams family group in 1873. Henry is standing on the left, his wife seated on the right.

saw his rival Jefferson's mansion at Monticello.

In 1788 Adams returned home where he was much admired for his labours in England. Everyone quoted his prescription for the new republic, "a government of laws and not of men." But like his descendants, Adams could never *not* express himself. In a lengthy treatise on the various American state constitutions, he made it plain that the country ought to be governed by "the rich, the well-born and the able". But the poor, the ill-born and the incompetent, that is to say the majority, disliked this bold elitism and Adams was to suffer to the end of his career gibes accusing him of being in favour of monarchy and aristocracy.

Democracy, Adams believed, was "the most ignoble and detestable form of government". The other Inventors agreed. But then, early on, they had a great fright. Before the separation from England only men of property could vote in Massachusetts. After independence, only men of property could vote in Massachusetts; but the property qualifications were doubled. A number of former soldiers led by one Daniel Shays revolted. Shays's Rebellion was quickly put down. The Inventors, however, now saw the need for a relatively strong Federal Constitution that would make 13 loosely allied states into a single nation with the sort of powers that would discourage rebellion and protect property. They also devised an Electoral College to choose president and vice-president. As expected, George Washington was unanimously elected president while the man who got the second most votes in the College became vice-president. On April 21, 1789, John Adams began the first of two terms as vice-president.

The early days of the American republic were dominated by England and France. The first American political parties were simply factions attached to one or the other of these two rich meddling and quarrelsome powers. Though Adams was sternly anti-English, he came to lead the Federalist or pro-British faction while Jefferson led the pro-French or Republican party. The Federalists included Washington, Hamilton, John Jay. The Republican leaders were Madison, Monroe, Burr. The Republican party approved of the French Revolution; the Federalists disliked it. The Republicans were for the most dominated by the Virginians, led by Jefferson with his dreams of an arcadia from which cities and manufactories and banks were excluded. But it was the Federalist Hamilton who saw the future plain and the United States today is very much the country that he wanted, and certainly predicted.

Nicknamed "his Rotundity", Adams presided over the Senate, and waited his turn to replace Washington.

That turn almost never came, thanks to Alexander Hamilton. In many ways the most brilliant as well as the most unstable of the Inventors, Hamilton was magically beguiling when he chose to be, particularly with doting older men like George Washington. During the eight years of Washington's presidency, secretary of the treasury Hamilton was, in effect, the actual ruler of the United States. Hamilton's pre-eminence did not please his senior in every sense, the Vice-President. Due to an untidy private life, foreign birth, and a personality calculated to make the ill-born froth with Jacobin sentiments, Hamilton was never himself a candidate for president. But he did his best to make Adams's elevation not the natural thing it ought to have been but a complicated near-miss with an unknown Southerner added to the ballot. Adams defeated Jefferson by only three votes.

In 1875 that glorious crook, contender for the presidency, and nobody's fool James G. Blaine was firmly opposed to the idea of nominating for president John Adams's grandson Charles Francis Adams. Blaine was firm: both President John Adams and his son President John Quincy Adams had each managed to kill his party. The Republican party of 1875 might be defeated and still survive, said Blaine, "but if it should win with Adams it would never live again". In one sense, this was very much a bum rap for the Adamses since their parties were, in any case, deteriorating. Yet it is true that their overwhelming *amour propre* was such that they were hopeless when it came to the greasy art of survival in American politics. Although they were sly enough to rise to the top, they were never sufficiently pliable to stay there.

John Adams began his presidency in a sour mood. He had nearly been robbed of the office by Hamilton. At the inaugural, Washington got all the attention: "He seemed to enjoy a triumph over me." The man he trusted least, the head of the Republican party, Thomas Jefferson was vice-president. Nevertheless, Adams decided to do his best to transcend faction, and so made the fatal mistake of retaining George Washington's Cabinet. This group of second-raters was for the most part loyal to Alexander Hamilton, now practising law at New York and dreaming of one day leading a great army into Mexico and South America in order to make himself another Bonaparte.

But for Hamilton to raise a great army he needed a war. After much intrigue, Hamilton nearly manoeuvred the United States into a war with France (one issue: Talleyrand had suggested that to keep the peace a bribe might be in order. Virtuous United Statesmen were outraged). The Republican party under Jefferson was not only pro-French but opposed to standing armies, taxes, and all the accoutrements of that nation-state which Hamilton saw as inevitable and desirable. Although Adams did his best to maintain the peace, Hamilton orchestrated the war-scare so skilfully that Adams was obliged to call Washington out of retirement to take charge of a mobilisation.

Ever obedient to the beloved Hamilton, Washington insisted that Adams make Hamilton the ranking major-general of the army: the national warlord. Overwhelmed by *force majeure* from Mount Vernon, Adams gave way. Hamilton could now attend Cabinet meetings; organise the coming war with France; and plan the eventual conquest of Latin America. But Adams was not without cunning. He continued to play up to the jingoes while quietly preparing an accommodation with France. Shortly before the election of 1800, the President's own minister to France made peace.

Finished as a party leader, Hamilton felt obliged to damage if not destroy Adams. With that creative madness for which he was noted, Hamilton wrote a 'secret' attack on the President while, quixotically, proposing that of course he be re-elected. Aaron Burr got a copy of Hamilton's pamphlet and published it, fatally splitting the Federalist party. Even so, had Burr not carried New York State for Jefferson and himself,

Adams would have been re-elected. As it was, he spent his last days in office at the new and dreadful 'city' of Washington, creating Federalist judges. The most significant act of John Adams's presidency was the appointment of John Marshall to be Chief Justice. More than any other Inventor, the conservative Marshall defined the United States and shaped its Constitution.

During the war-scare, the infamous Alien and Sedition acts were passed by a panicky Congress, and Adams had the bad sense to sign them. In effect, they suspended freedom of speech "in the national interest", as the Nixonians would say. Historians have tended to be overwhelmed by this blot on the Adams administration (yet hardly any historian, retrospectively, much minds the fact that the sainted Lincoln suspended *habeas corpus* in the Civil War). Actually, it was not the high-handed attitude towards civil rights that harmed the Federalists but, as John Quincy Adams wrote, "The (creation of) the army was the first decisive symptom of a schism in the Federal Party itself, which accomplished its final overthrow and that of the administration."

Refusing to remain in Washington for the inauguration of his successor Thomas Jefferson, Adams went home to Massachusetts where he lived for another 26

Henry, great-grandson of John Adams, novelist, autobiographer, and one of America's great historians.

years. Towards the end of his life he conducted a fascinating correspondence with Jefferson that does credit to both. Each died on the same day, July 4, 1826.

Summing up his own career, Adams wrote, "I cannot repent of anything I ever did conscientiously and from a sense of duty. I never engaged in public affairs for my own interest, pleasure, envy, jealousy, avarice, ambition, or even the desire of fame." Excepting 'pleasure' and perhaps 'avarice', Adams listed his own peculiar faults. Nevertheless, despite ambition, envy, etc., Adams acted well and his rationalisation for his failure as President rings true: "If any of these (faults) had been my motive, my conduct would have been very different." Certainly he was no mere opportunist; and he believed that his best act was the one that cost him re-election: "I desire no other inscription over my gravestone than: 'Here lies John Adams, who took upon himself the responsibility of the peace with France in the year 1800'." In the mantelpiece of the dining room at the White House is carved a line from one of Adam's letters to his wife, "May none but honest and wise men ever rule under this roof".

When John Adams ceased to be President, his son John Quincy Adams was 33 years old, and the ablest of America's diplomats. In 1791 John Quincy was at London, helping John Jay negotiate a treaty. Although John Quincy was now too grand to stoop to hypergamy, he did manage to bring into the family a new type: he married Louisa Johnson, the daughter of the American consul general at London. Mr Johnson was a distinguished Marylander married to an English woman. Brought up in Europe, Louisa was "charming, like a Romney portrait", according to her grandson Henry Adams, "but among her many charms that of being a New England woman was not one". Louisa did not take to Boston, Braintree, Quincy ("Had I stepped into Noah's Ark, I do not think I could have been more utterly astonished"). Happily, the old President took to her. She also made John Quincy a good wife; but then great men seldom make bad marriages.

John Quincy disliked the idea of holding diplomatic posts under his father. Uncharacteristically, Washington himself wrote to the new President John Adams expressing the hope, "that you will not withhold merited promotion from Mr John (Quincy) Adams because he is your son". So John Quincy Adams was posted American minister to Prussia 1797–1801. He then returned to Boston ostensibly to practise law but, actually, to become the president. He served as a commissioner in bankruptcy until removed by President Jefferson (who later, disingenuously, denied any knowledge of this petty act against the son of his predecessor). After service in the state legislature, John

Quincy was sent to the United States Senate in 1803; as senator, he showed a complete independence of party, supporting Jefferson's Embargo Act. As the saying went, "the Republicans trampled upon the Federalists, and the Federalists trampled upon John Quincy Adams".

Personally, John Quincy was esteemed but not much liked. He himself liked neither political party: "between both, I see the impossibility of pursuing the dictates of my own conscience, without sacrificing every prospect, not merely of advancement, but even of retaining that character and reputation I have enjoyed. Yet my own choice is made, and if I cannot hope to give satisfaction to my country, I am at least determined to have the approbation of my own reflections."

But presently John Quincy gave satisfaction both to country and self. Once again the stage was England. After losing his seat in the Senate, he served four years as President Madison's minister to Russia during the War of 1812 (a war not celebrated by the English who seem to have forgotton that their troops burned the capital city while President Madison roamed forlornly about the countryside, trying to find his government). In 1814 John Quincy Adams was appointed one of the commissioners to make peace with England, the meetings to be held at Ghent.

Among the other four commissioners were the brilliant Albert Gallatin, the Geneva-born secretary of the treasury to Jefferson, and the rising Kentucky lawyer and quadrennial presidential candidate Henry Clay. The five men shared the same house in Ghent. Clay wanted to sit up all night and gamble while Adams liked to go to bed at nine; wild oats seem never to have been planted (at least visibly) in the garden of any Adams. John Quincy particularly avoided actresses "because", he writes touchingly in old age, "the first woman I ever loved was an actress, but I never spoke to her, and I think I never saw her off the stage . . . Of all the ungratified longings that I ever suffered, that of being acquainted with her, merely to tell her how much I adored her, was the most intense." At the time this Laura and Petrarch were each 14 years old. The Puritan must suffer or he is not good.

The English peace negotiators proved to be so inadequate that Lord Castlereagh asked in the House, "Whether the persons sent . . . for the American government were quite forgotten by His Majesty's Ministers, or whether anyone had been appointed to treat with them?"

Clay had been as responsible as any American leader for the war with England (he particularly wanted to annex Canada); consequently, he was quite

Charles Francis Adams II (left), Union officer, writer, later President of the Union Pacific Railroad.

willing to prolong the war in order "to make us a warlike people". But John Quincy was not a warlover; he also knew that the English Ministry was not happy with a war that could not be won, particularly at a time when not only had Castlereagh managed to antagonise both Russia and Prussia but Lord Liverpool's Government was being much criticised for imposing a property tax in order to prosecute a far-off war. On December 24, 1814, the treaty of Ghent was signed. Two weeks later, a wild Tennessee backwoodsman named Andrew Jackson won a mighty victory over English troops at New Orleans. The fact that the war was already over made the victory no less sweet for the humiliated Americans, and the political star of Jackson was now in the ascendant.

Like his father before him, John Quincy Adams was appointed minister to England. For two years the Adamses lived at Ealing, then a country town. They were pressed for money, which was just as well for they were not much sought after by London society. For one thing, Americans of any kind were less than the vogue; for another, Adamses can never be in vogue. But John Quincy's eye was as sharp as ever. Of Castlereagh, he wrote, "his manner was cold, but not absolutely repulsive". He did enjoy Holland House and what intellectual company came his way. Meanwhile, his son Charles Francis Adams was initiated to the glories and miseries of the English public school where being an American was not a passport to gentle treatment. The mark of an English schooling on Charles Francis Adams's character was life-long, and perhaps saved the nation from a third Adams presidency.

Meanwhile, John Quincy had become a Republican. The old Federalist party had fallen apart. Everyone was now a Republican of one sort or another. The Western leader of the party was Henry Clay, closely pressed by Andrew Jackson. John Quincy himself was not a man of locality: "my system of politics more and more inclines to strengthen the union and the government." Yet when he heard an American jingo say, as a toast, "Our country, right or wrong," John Quincy responded severely: "I disclaim all patriotism incompatible with the principles of eternal justice." It never occurred, as far as we know, to any Adams of the Four Generations that there might be no such thing as eternal justice. The first Adams believed in the Puritan God. The second was equally devout. In the last generation overt religion vanished almost entirely in their voluminous letters and diaries; nevertheless, the idea of eternal justice, of moral right, of some essential and binding law to the universe never ceased to order their lives.

President Monroe appointed John Quincy to be his secretary of state, at that time the second most important office in the land and the surest way to the presidency. The eight years that John Quincy served President Monroe was known as the era "of good feelings". It was indeed a tribute to John Quincy's pronounced excellence that he was given the post for Monroe was a Virginian and the Virginians had governed the United States from the beginning: Washington, Jefferson, Madison and Monroe dominated the nation for 36 years with only one break, the four years that John Adams of Massachusetts was president.

John Quincy was not delighted with Cabinet life: "There is a slowness, want of decision, and a spirit of procrastination in the President, which perhaps arises more from his situation than his personal character." Experiencing flak from the ambitious Clay and his other rivals for the presidency Jackson and Crawford, John Quincy wrote, "My office . . . makes it for the interest of all the partisans of the candidates for the next Presidency . . . to decry me as much as possible". "Always complain, but superbly explain" could be the Adams family motto.

General Andrew Jackson meanwhile was on the rampage in the Spanish Floridas, hanging people right and left, including two Englishmen. Yet John Quincy did his best to defend Jackson (a man of whom Jefferson wrote, Now he is *really* crazy!), and in the process formulated what is known as the Monroe Doctrine: that no European power may interfere in the Western hemisphere; while no American government will interfere in Europe. This proud doctrine is still, theoretically, in force although it was abrogated in 1917 when the United States went to war with Germany.

Jackson's filibuster-capers appealed hugely to the electorate and in 1824, under the system of the Electoral College, Jackson received 99 votes for president; Adams, 84; Crawford, 41; Clay, 37. Since no candidate had the required majority, the election went into the House of Representatives for decision. Rightly,

Clay feared Jackson, the hero of New Orleans, more than he did John Quincy. Clay gave his support to John Quincy Adams who became president in February 1825. Clay was then appointed secretary of state. Everyone cried "foul", and John Quincy was held to be corrupt by all Jackson men and a good many disinterested worthies as well. Now, once again, there was a President Adams; and he proved to be every bit as wounded in his *amour propre,* as bitter as the first Adams who wrote from Massachusetts: "My dear son, never did I feel so much solemnity as upon this occasion. The multitude of my thoughts, and the intensity of my feelings are too much for a mind, like mine, in its 90th year."

The administration of John Quincy Adams proved to be even more of a disaster (for him) than that of his father. Jackson and his allies were rightly indignant at losing an election in which Jackson had, after all, got the most votes; they also regarded as corrupt the alliance between John Quincy and Clay. Nor did the new President very much like or understand the country he presided over. For one thing, democracy had made a sudden advance with universal suffrage (that is, any free man over 21 could now vote) and the rule by the best was ended once and for all.

John Quincy saw what was coming but he meant to hold the line, and his first inaugural address was a challenge to the democrats: "While foreign nations, less blessed with that freedom which is power than ourselves" (obligatory gesture to Demos) "are advancing with gigantic strides in the career of public improvements, are we to slumber in our indolence or fold up our arms and proclaim to the world that we are *palsied by the will of our constituents?*" There sounded for the last time *ex cathedra presidentis,* the voice of the original Inventors of the nation.

John Quincy had great plans to foster education, science, commerce, civil service reform; but his projects were too rigorous and too un-political to be accepted. For instance, the United States had not one astronomical station while in Europe there were 130 "lighthouses of the sky". This happy phrase was received with perfect derision by the mob. It was plain that John Quincy was not suited to lead a quasi-democracy. He was too intelligent, too unyielding, too tactless. He also found hard to bear the inanities of political attack (he was supposed to have supplied a lecherous Russian nobleman with an innocent American girl). Needless to say, Jackson swamped him in the next election. The Jackson slogan was prophetic of the new era: "Jackson who can fight, and Adams who can write."

"Three days more, and I shall be restored to private

life . . . I go into it with a combination of parties and of public men against my character and reputation such as I believe never before was exhibited . . ." Pure Adams, the self pity; but not so far off the mark.

Like his father, John Quincy Adams refused to attend the inaugural of his successor. Back in Massachusetts, he started to put his father's papers in order but this bookish task bored him. He was not cut out for libraries and retirement. To the horror of his son Charles Francis Adams, John Quincy "demeaned" himself and went back to Washington as a mere representative to Congress where he served in the House until his death 17 years later. As Emerson rather unexpectedly wrote, "Mr Adams chose wisely and according to his constitution, when, on leaving the presidency, he went into Congress. He is no literary old gentleman, but a bruiser, and he loves the *mêlée* . . . He is an old *roué* who cannot live on slops, but must have sulphuric acid in his tea."

Certainly John Quincy Adams's most useful period was the last when he was obliged to enter the hurly-burly at something of a disadvantage. For one thing, his voice was weak, his manner tentative: "It is so long since I was in the habit of speaking to a popular assembly, and I am so little qualified by nature for an extemporaneous orator, that I was at the time not a little agitated by the sound of my own voice." But he persisted, fighting and eventually winning the battle to admit those petitions against slavery that the House would not for years entertain. He helped create the Smithsonian Institute. He denounced the American conquest of Mexico which added Texas and California to the empire. Then, in the midst of a debate, he collapsed on the floor of the House; he was taken to the Speaker's chambers. On February 23, 1848, he died. Final words: "This is the last of earth. I am content."

The Third Generation was on the rise. Charles Francis Adams had committed hypergamy in the sense that he was the first Adams to marry a great deal of money in the shape of Abigail Brooks who, according to one of her children, took a "constitutional and sincere pleasure in the forecast of evil. She delighted in the dark side of anticipation." Four of her sons were to be remarkable in the next generation: John Quincy II, Charles Francis II, Henry and Brooks. Like all the Adamses the sons were voluminous writers and Henry was a writer of genius (although his brother Charles wrote rather better prose). Their father also wrote copiously or, as his son Charles observed glumly, while writing his father's biography: "He took to diary writing early, and he took to it bad." Mark Twain apologised to William Dean Howells for using

John Quincy Adams II, politician who turned Democrat.

"three words where one would answer – a thing I am always trying to guard against. I shall become as slovenly a writer as Charles Francis Adams if I don't look out . . ."

It is during the Fourth Generation that the high moral style of the early and the puissant Adamses is now tinged with irony, that necessary weapon of the power-less. There was to be no more life at the very top for the family but there were still good, even great things to be done.

Of his father Charles Francis Adams, Henry wrote, "(his) memory was hardly above the average; his mind was not bold like his grandfather's or restless like his father's, or imaginative, or oratorical – still less mathematical; but it worked with singular perfection . . . Within its range it was a model." The range included diplomacy and the by now inevitable family post of minister at London. Charles Francis was minister during the difficult years 1861-68 when a powerful movement in England favoured the Confederacy for reasons both sentimental and practical. The despised colonies of four-score years before had now become a predatory and dangerous empire, filling up the North American continent and threatening, by its existence, the British Empire. The vision of the United States split into two countries brought roses to many a cheek both on the government and the opposition benches.

Adams went about his work of keeping England neutral with that coolness which had caused a political associate to describe him as "the greatest Iceberg in the Northern Hemisphere". This solemn gelidity was now transferred to 5 Upper Portland Place where, the minister remarked, "My practice has been never to manifest feeling of any kind, either of elation or of depression. In this, some Englishmen have taken occasion to intimate that I have been thought quite successful."

The position of the English Ministry tended to shift with the fortunes of war. At first, the South appeared to be winning; then the North. Working-class sentiment was pro-Northern despite considerable unemployment brought on by the Northern blockade of the South's ports, preventing the English from importing cotton. Charles Francis did not have much to do with the working classes but he did find support and solace from, variously, Monckton Milnes, the Duke of Argyll, Cobden and Bright.

Paradoxically, much of the pro-Southern sentiment in England came from those who abominated the peculiar institution of slavery. Although they disapproved of the slave-holding South, they saw Lincoln as a ruthless despot, trying to hold together by force a union that was constitutionally based on the right of any state to leave that union when it chose. Lincoln was never, to say the least, devoted to the abolition of slavery; and not until the war to preserve the union had gone on for two years did he free the slaves. Consequently Charles Francis was forced to listen to much sharp criticism from high-minded anti-slave Englishmen while his son Henry (acting as the minister's secretary) was denounced in the street for Lincoln's wickedness by Thackeray.

The chief crisis in Anglo-American relations during Charles Francis's ministry was the *Alabama* affair. *The Alabama* was a formidable warship built at Liverpool for the South. Charles Francis maintained that if the English allowed such a ship to be built and armed, they automatically ceased to be neutral. The Foreign Secretary Lord John Russell asked for proof of the ship's ultimate use. When this was provided, the Attorney General supported Charles Francis and recommended that the ship be seized. But by then *The Alabama* had sailed, embarrassing Palmerston's Government. The American minister then proceeded to keep careful count of each ship sunk by *The Alabama* in the course of the war and later saw to it that England paid the bill.

Undaunted, the Southerners continued to build warships at Liverpool, placing their orders through a French firm supposedly representing the Pasha of Egypt. Had the South got these ships they would have been in a position to blockade Boston and New York. Charles Francis again protested to Lord John who was reasonably sympathetic, or as the minister wrote in his diary: "Russell is too old and skilful a politician not to understand the necessity, for his own security, of keeping the minds of his countrymen free from all suspicion of being superfluously courteous to any foreign power."

But when the first ship was ready to go to sea and Lord John seemed unwilling to stop it, Adams then played the diplomat's ultimate card. He re-stated his case; he then declared that should the Government allow the ship in question to sail, "it would be superfluous in me to point out to your lordship that this is war". Three days later Lord John seized (and eventually bought) the Southern warships. Actually, the Prime Minister had wanted from the beginning, as a matter of policy, to keep the ships out of Confederate hands but could not (and never did) find a correct legal formula.

Now the focus shifts to the Fourth Generation. Henry Adams in his autobiography *The Education of Henry Adams* (where he refers to himself in the third person) writes a good deal about his formative years in London as his father's secretary. Although there is little doubt that Henry inherited the family passion to be the first in the nation, it was already plain to him that the great plutocratic democracy was not apt to take well to one with such an 'education'. The age of the robber barons was now in full swing. Shysters like Jay Gould and Jim Fisk controlled the economic life of the country, buying and selling members of Congress (and presidents). Although Henry's father was, from time to time, mentioned for president (and was actually on the ticket of a splinter party), no-one ever took very seriously this brilliant, cold man who spoke French better than English.

Of the four sons of Charles Francis only John Quincy Adams II wanted a career in politics. He even became a Democrat; but he did not go very far. Uniquely, John Quincy II tried to get out from under the weight of the family's intellectual tradition by, among other things, abandoning "the vile family habit of preserving letters". His father, on the other hand, was not only happy among the thousands of Adams letters, diaries, notebooks but spent the remainder of his life trying to order them.

The second son Charles Francis II was a marvellous scribbler; also, a man of action. After examining in detail the misdeeds of the railroad tycoons (published in a volume called *Chapters of Erie*, with several essays by his brother Henry), he himself became a railroad tycoon, and president of the Union Pacific. The next brother Henry was to write the finest of American histories, dealing with the administrations of his father's rival Jefferson and of Jefferson's successor Madison. Henry also wrote one of America's few good political novels, *Democracy*. The younger brother Brooks was also a writer very much in the Adams (by now) highly pessimistic vein. In fact, it is he who rather gives the game away with the title he chose for a posthumous edition of some of his brother Henry's essays, *The Degradation of the Democratic Dogma*.

* * * * *

I cannot remember when I was not fascinated by Henry Adams. I was brought up in Washington; belonged to a political family; and used often to pass the site of the house where Adams had lived in Lafayette Park, just opposite the White House.

Once I asked Eleanor Roosevelt if she had known Henry Adams (he died in 1918). "Oh, yes! He was such a kind man, so good with the children. They would crawl all over him when he sat in his Victoria. He was very . . . tolerant. But," and she frowned, "we did *not* agree politically. I remember the first time we went to his house. My Franklin had just come to Washington" (as assistant secretary of the navy) "and I of course was very shy then and could never get the courage to speak up, particularly with someone so much older. Well, my Franklin made some remark about President Wilson, about how well he was doing. And Mr Adams just laughed at him and pointed towards the White House and said, 'Young man, it doesn't make the slightest difference who lives in that house, history goes on with or without the president.' Well, I just couldn't keep quiet. 'Mr Adams,' I said, 'that is a very terrible thing to say to a young man who wants to go into politics and be of use to other people.' Oh, I made quite a speech." "And what did Mr Adams say?" "I can't remember. I think he just laughed at me. We were always good friends."

So the great Adams line ended with a theory of history that eliminated Carlyle's hero and put in its stead something like Hegel's "course of the divine life". Yet one can see from the beginning the family's dependency on fate, on some inscrutable power at work in the universe which raised men up or cut them down, and guided nations. At the beginning this was, plainly, the work of the Puritan God. Later, when that God failed, it was simply energy or 'the Dynamo', as Henry Adams called those "secret invisible Laws of Nature" that hurl this petty race through time and spinning space.

There was a degree of sourness in Henry's old age;

after all, he was living across the park from the White House where grandfather and great-grandfather had presided. As compensation, his beautiful memoir is filled with a good deal of mock humility, confessions of 'failure', and a somewhat over-wrought irony. "I like [Henry]," wrote Henry James, "but suffer from his monotonous, disappointed pessimism . . . However, when the poor dear is in London, I don't fail to do what I can." Yet, politically, Henry Adams was not without influence; his best friend and next-door neighbour was that most literary of secretaries of state John Hay, while Adams himself was always at the centre of the capital's intellectual life. Invitations to his house were much sought after; yet he "called on no-one, and never left a card". Henry James in a short story set in Washington describes a distinguished figure based on Henry Adams. As the character draws up a guest list for a party, he says, finally, wearily: "Well, why not be vulgar? Let us ask the President."

Henry Adams was remarkably prescient about the coming horrors, and like his mother anticipated the worst. Before the First World War, he prophesied the decline of England and France, and the rise of the United States, Russia and Germany. But in the long run, he felt that Germany was too small a power "to swing the club". Ultimately, he saw the world in two blocs: the east dominated by Russia; the west dominated by the United States. He also predicted that should Russia and China ever come together "the result will be a single mass which no amount of force could possibly deflect". He predicted that this great mass would be both socialist and despotic; and its only counterbalance would be an "Atlantic combine", stretching from "the Rocky mountains on the west to the Elbe on the east". Because of this vision, Adams always used what influence he had to try to persuade the various American administrations to bring Russia into their sphere of influence. But he was ahead of his time . . . unusual for an Adams since their usual time was always some golden age of virtue just passed.

The last days of Henry Adams were spent trying to understand the forces that control history. He wanted an equivalent in history to Einstein's much sought after (but never found) unified field theory. The best Henry Adams could do was a chapter of his memoir called *A Dynamic Theory of History*; and it was not enough. Finally, Adams abandoned history altogether. "I don't give a damn what happened," he wrote, "what I want to know is why it happened – never could find out – stopped writing history."

One can hear John Adams's response to that: "History is to be Made not Written despite the Malice and Envy of Opponents and of Faction . . ."

VANDERBILT

V. S. Pritchett

Opposite: the founder of an empire – Cornelius Vanderbilt I, the Commodore.

Above left and centre: 'Commodore' Vanderbilt's mother Phebe, and the house at Stapleton, Staten Island, where he was born. Above right: his second wife Frank, a distant relative fifty years younger than him. Top: Abraham Lincoln (in the foreground, right) and the Commodore (seated, in top hat) at Saratoga Springs in the 1860s; the Commodore lent his ship, *The Vanderbilt*, to the North during the Civil War. Right: the richest man in America – the Commodore in old age, with one of his grandchildren.

"Clogs to clogs in three generations," they used to say when Lancashire was rich. In the United States the proverb is more genteel – "shirt sleeves to shirt sleeves". When 120 of the descendants of Cornelius Vanderbilt, 'the Commodore' and founder of the family, met in 1973 for the first tribal reunion in their history, at Vanderbilt University in Tennessee, there would have been no need to sing the handsome old Robber Baron's favourite hymn *Come ye sinners poor and needy*. (It had been sung at his deathbed in Washington Square nearly 100 years before.) The days of the Vanderbilt mansions, copied from French châteaux, on Fifth Avenue, were over. The other mansions at Newport and the feudal estate at Asheville had gone, along with the maroon coloured breeches and white stockings of the footmen, but need was not the note of the day.

The gathering appeared to be now a group of comfortable middle-class people, mainly in the professions and not inclined for splash; here and there one could detect the Vanderbilt good looks. If the statue of the famous rough old Commodore could have stumbled out a speech one can imagine he would have uttered some of the cuss words he had picked up as a youth when he was a 'harbour rat' in New York harbour in the 1820s. He might have asked 'how come' so few of the Vanderbilts knew one another? Where were the steamship lines? Where was the railway empire that had knit a chaotic country together? Why had his dull son, William Henry, forgotten the oath he had made to his father and split a fortune into 32 warring parts? Why had God decreed that in every generation they should produce an unconscionable number of girls who scatter family fortunes? Where was dynasty? True, his descendants were a sporting lot. They liked speed and racing. One had won the America's Cup and had soothed the savage breasts of clubmen by inventing Contract Bridge – the Commodore had liked a game of cards himself. And there was this University. He didn't mind admitting he had left school at 11. On one of his trips to Europe the Commodore had noticed that dukes and lords could speak more fluently than he could himself, but he had had to be *pushed* into founding the place when he was weak and old and it was a long way from New York. As he surveyed the family he would be struck by the painful fact that there was not a millionaire among them. He had made his millions in 15 years, whereas it had taken snobs like the Astors two generations; yet in the millionaire stakes the Vanderbilts had fallen from the top to a low place in the second ranks of wealth, easily out-paced by the Rockefellers, the du Ponts and the Fords.

32   The Vanderbilts were Dutch. The earliest American ancestor was said to be Jan Aertsen from one of the Dutch *bilts* – the name for higher land in Holland. The Dutch knew one another by their Christian names and Jan Aertsen would be no more than a peasant from such a piece of land. He had crossed the Atlantic as an immigrant to the new colony founded by the Dutch West India Company when the Dutch were at the height of their maritime power and political enlightenment, an able well-governed money-minded people, the closest rivals to the English in trade. They were a race of born bankers, sea-going merchants, canal and river traders and busy market gardeners, and when the Company shrewdly built their entrepôt, their windmills and their forts at the toe of Manhattan, they had not only chosen perhaps the largest deep water harbour on the Atlantic coast, but one which topographically must have reminded them of home.

Imagination was not the Dutch gift, but an inch by inch foresight was. Manhattan lay between the politically high-minded colonies in Philadelphia and New England and was indifferent to metaphysics and witches. It was more than content to hold the key to overseas and inland trade, in a seaport that could not help become richer every year; it was not a place for manufacture, but for import-export, fur-carriers, collecting other people's money at the chief gateway to the New World. The canny ones left the farms they had cut out of the forests in the valleys between the chocolate-coloured rocks and went to the waterside of the little town. Its streets were tangled and dirty, the pigs did the scavenging, the water was bad; but there were 2000 negro slaves to wait on one and empty the sewage into the harbour. The money-minded could soon live sumptuously, hold a sort of merchant Court and give the roaring parties they loved.

One branch of the Jan Aertsen family who had farmed at Flatbush on Long Island had done this and were soon well-established. But there was a dull, plodding strain in the Bilts or Derbilts, as they came to call themselves, and this branch broke off to settle on the little triangle of Staten Island at the entrance to the harbour. It was a safe place, had a small garrison but, as far as hope of fortune was concerned, was cut off by five miles of water from the tip of Manhattan. Some colonists on Staten Island had small estates among the hills, but the Derbilts became poorer and stagnant: they made a hard living as market gardeners and eked it out by ferrying and fishing.

The first hint of awakening on Staten Island came when the Moravians from Holland built a church there; working on the job was enough to convert the Derbilts and they were prodded by the missionary into building boats to bring over more Moravians from Holland. One of these boat-building market gardeners and ferrymen was Cornelius Derbilt, a handsome simple fellow. And with him, or rather because of his young wife, Phebe Hand, the poor Derbilts stirred in their long sleep. She was not a Staten islander nor was she Dutch. She was of English descent and had been sent across the river from New Jersey as a child when New Jersey became a battlefield, to live and work in a clergyman's family. Her own people had once had money. They had been split in their loyalties: Phebe Hand's father was a prosperous Tory; her uncle was a Major General in Washington's Army. Her own small inheritance had vanished in Revolutionary notes, but she was independent and spirited enough to side with the rebels. She is spoken of as a lively, rather mannish, caustic, war-time girl, a devil for work and with an eye for money. She married Cornelius in the 1790s to get out of the clergyman's house and from her will-power, her foresight and her 'sparing', the later Vanderbilts piously date the spectacular rise in their fortunes. Her second son, another Cornelius, but called Corneel, and the fourth of her nine children was to become the Commodore and the millionaire.

In the history of the Vanderbilts from this generation onwards there is a repeated and extreme conflict between fathers and sons, a conflict common enough in the 19th century. Part ferryman, part farmer on a tiny farm, Phebe Hand's husband slaved with her and the rest of the children and was content and easily gulled: she had to get his money off him before he was tricked out of it. By the time he was 11 and after the death of his elder brother, her second son Corneel began to take the lead in the family. He refused to stay at school. His eyes were on the harbour and the sails that crowded it – from the sea-going schooners, frigates and the privateers to his father's periauger, a copy of the heavy barges used on the Dutch canals. Corneel was down at the waterside just after dawn to hear his father blow his conch shell to call the passengers, then off father and son sailed to the tip of Manhattan with passengers, loads of hay, vegetables or fish. Sometimes they rowed or poled the heavy boat in the shallow or tricky channels, racing the rival ferries to be first at the market and catch the high prices. There they had to waste time all day which drove the boy mad – he was soon trying to argue his father into going over to Brooklyn – at last there was the two hour journey back, often after dark, on the difficult tack home.

In time Corneel spent less and less time drudging for his father on the land, more and more on the boat, until he was allowed to take it on his own. The work was heavy; the only boyish diversion was in racing the rival ferries, but the harder the work the more he enjoyed it, the more he wanted a periauger of his own, for he saw that his strength surpassed his father's and he loved the rough life. At the age of 17 he could stand working for the old man no longer. He threatened to go to sea if his mother could not open the kitchen clock where she kept the family savings and lend him 100 dollars to buy his boat. He promised to pay her back in a year. Phebe Hand was a good-humoured woman but she liked a hard deal. She offered him the money on conditions that were almost impossible: he had to plough eight acres of their land before his birthday at the end of the month. Tom Sawyer-like he bribed and cajoled the local lads into doing most of the job for him, got his boat and, in the standard fashion of American success stories, came back with a profit of 1000 dollars at the end of the year and handed it to his mama.

The character of Corneel was formed. Americans often complain that they have no childhood: Corneel certainly had none and did not want it. He had known only work, and hard work had increased an energy already remarkable. When he looked at the sails in the harbour they were not merely pretty sails as they blew across, they were making money. He paid what he made into the family, indeed he was soon largely supporting them. He did not resent this. He went out day and night to make more, to exploit the harbour and get shares in other periaugers.

He had grown into a bronzed and handsome six-footer with strong shoulders, straw coloured hair, shrewd half-closed blue eyes and by the time he was nineteen the open softness of youth had gone. He was hard of tongue, ignorant, defiant, rough yet drily humorous. His boisterous swearing served to hide what was in his mind and was also a noise that expressed what he could not put into ordinary language. He was already a stubborn take-it-or-leave-it young man. Mockers feared his fists; he was honest and was known for doing what he promised and for being blunt with his betters, the solid merchants of the old New York stock and new men like Astor who had risen from nothing but were already making a fortune in buying up and building. If the pursuit of money – a word which even today in New York speech seems to begin with a stressed double 'm' – had not ruled Corneel's mind, New York itself would have made it do so. But the New Yorkers made a good deal of their money out of speculation; Corneel's cautious nature rejected that. What his training on the periauger taught him was that he had hit on a trade where there was no risk: people were restless: like himself they were always on

34

en the Commodore
d in 1877, most of his
une went to his son
liam Henry, a shrewd
ruthless businessman
ose uncompromising
tudes to his workers
de him one of the most
opular men in the land,
these contemporary
toons imply. When he
l, only eight years
r his father, his skilful
dling of the family
pire had made him the
est man in the world.

the move from place to place. He was the carrier who would take them and much farther than the trip from Staten Island to Whitehall Steps. The more the city grew, the farther they went: the Hudson, the harbour, the sounds, the maze of river water round Manhattan were almost the only roads. Every American knew that America was geography; every American was grandiloquent about it. The taciturn young Vanderbilt knew that geography was money.

At nineteen there was another conflict with his father. Corneel married his first cousin, Sophia Johnson, a girl as unlike the flighty girls he saw in New York as possible; a timid but sturdy girl who lived almost next door. Her looks recommended her: she looked like his mother, being the daughter of his mother's sister. There was a battle because his parents believed that a marriage of first cousins would certainly produce an idiot. Corneel was not a man to trust anyone outside the family. He seems to have married for love, but for more to dispose of nature. If Sophia looked like his mother she had not the mother's character. Sophia was no better educated than he was. She was not the girl who would stand up to a husband who was already a restless, driving egotist. However, he got the work out of her as he did out of himself: she bore him thirteen children.

The marriage was a working marriage. Corneel was out with his boats all the week. When the War of 1812 came he was quick to see that if it ruined New York trade it would set him on to fortune. The harbour was blockaded, the town was in a panic fearing attack and starvation; only the harbour boatmen could bring the food down the Hudson into the town. The gamblers plumped for the big money by going outside the Narrows as privateers and running the blockade, but many lost their ships and ended up as prisoners of the British. Corneel was too fly to take that risk. He bought a large periauger called *Dread* and brought food down from the farms of the Hudson. Prices were high and what with that and getting a solid contract for taking out supplies to the garrison, he slyly avoided being called up to the militia. He made a small fortune – by his standards, not by those of New York – and when the War was over he had enough to buy a partnership in a ramshackle schooner. His map grew larger. In the winter when his periauger was locked in the ice of New York harbour he was off with whale oil, woollens, wine and spirits to Virginia, picking up cargoes of timber to bring back. In the summer he was trading in fruit and fish right up to Albany. On one venture he took 30,000 shad to New Brunswick and when he found he could not sell them there he got men to go out on the country roads and peddle them

The Vanderbilt house at New Brunswick, New Jersey.

inland. By now he could afford to leave a young brother to take over the job of supporting his parents and put his own money into more boats. By the age of 24, in 1818, and as frugal as his mother had been, he had put by 9000 dollars.

Sail still crowded the harbour, but steamer smoke was now blowing across it. Fulton's paddle boat, *The Clermont*, had gone up the Hudson at two knots before the War of 1812; now others operating under exclusive New York State licence were splashing and stinking their way up to Albany or connecting with Philadelphia. Under steam, passengers could now get out of New York by the Raritan river to New Brunswick in nine hours, take the stage coach to Trenton where they picked up the superb Delaware river for the rest of the journey. Corneel had a sailor's contempt for steamers; they caught fire or their boilers blew up – B'ilers, he called them – they plodded where sail cut along. It is, at first sight, strange that an ambitious man should be slow to take up with the new thing; but he was not by nature an innovator. He was a cautious water peasant still and, perhaps in the hard work and exhilaration of sail he found a simple outlet for his huge physical power. Sail was the nearest thing to a childhood he had ever had. (Later on in life he was to hate railways until the money in them was irresistible.) Without schooling, he learned by rule of thumb, inching his way: he planned slowly and liked the power of being his own master and driving others on low wages as he drove himself for small profits and putting them by. His rise to power as a business man owed much to having an eye to everything, a head with a command of detail, the ability to keep quiet about what he was doing and an astute fighter's sense of timing that would put him one step ahead of his competitors at the right moment. There was yet another reason for his delay: he was bored by his young family and his timid wife and at a loss. He judged them as he judged others, by himself: how hard could they work? His family were contributing nothing.

Suddenly his slow mind gave a leap. He reversed or appeared to reverse, his character. He threw up his independence and at twenty-six went to work, at a poor salary, for a steamboat owner in New Brunswick and put his wife and children to work. The arrangement had cunning in it. New Brunswick was the port, as I have said, where steamer passengers changed for the stage coach. They were obliged to stay the night at an inn before going on next day by the Delaware to Philadelphia, a city at the time far more important than New York. The inn, he saw, was the pot of gold. He rented the worst inn in the town but one which had the advantage of being close to the landing stage, put his wife there to clean it up and run it. Under his contract the ship owner furnished the place and Corneel took all the profits. As for the boat, he was content to be an ill-paid captain but he laid down the policy: he would make war on the New York monopoly by cutting rates from four dollars to one for the trip and make up the loss by charging high prices for food and drink at the bar. It was agreed that half of these profits were his.

The venture was a huge success. Passengers crowded in. His wife was an excellent innkeeper. Her complaining stopped. The children carried in the baggage. And, behind the success, was the very American love of cunning and illegality for he was fighting competitors who had the law on their side. He was out of reach of New York State law in New Jersey: in New York waters he was a pirate. Of course, the Monopoly put the law on him but he was up to a dozen tricks. He had a secret cabin in his boat, *The Bellona*, where he hid when officials came aboard to arrest him. At other times he tricked them by proving that on this occasion, he was not in fact the captain or that the boat had another owner. He discovered the delights of outwitting them. To this excitement there was another lure: racing – the future passion of all Vanderbilts. The competing steamer captains loved to squeeze the greatest speed out of their boats. They tied down the safety valves to keep up steam almost to the point of explosion. And in one particular Corneel's boat – and others he was soon commanding – was original, for he had gone into the question of

boilers thoroughly. To get the utmost drive out of a boiler he saw it must be close to the paddles and under the feet of the captain: no rushing off and losing time in giving orders. Corneel stood at the wheel and tapped his orders to the engineer below, in code, with his walking stick. One has the impression that, after bad language, the tapping stick was to become his lifelong mode of conversation.

Soon the Monopoly, who failed to catch him on the river or trap him in the State Court at Albany, tried to bribe him. He replied – according to one of his biographers, A. Howden Smith – that his boss treated him squarely. "I don't keer so much 'bout makin' money as I do 'bout makin' my p'int and comin' out ahead." It is Tom Sawyer or Huck Finn speaking.

In 1827 Cornelius van DerBilt – as he now signed himself – was thirty-three, a hard, enjoyable 'character' among the racing river captains. Working at a poor salary but piling up the fringe benefits he was having the happiest time in his life. The inn, called Bellona Hall, was known for its good food and lodging. He had built a house for his wife and children in order to make a bit more by letting the rooms they had occupied at the inn. He had made money for his boss and 30,000 dollars for himself. His boss, who was a banker at heart, offered to sell him the Line and he could easily have raised the money and settled in New Brunswick for good, for he loved the restless up-and-down river life: his ideal was never to be much in his own home. He was certainly not of the domestic kind. When he got back home he was soon out and spending his violent physical energy on racing trotters and taking up with women at the little resort, keeping his mind sharp in card-playing and letting himself go with the whisky bottle; but these things were not careers. Money existed for the purpose of making more. Not to know that was to ignore the deepest instinct of the Founding Fathers, to ignore the map of the Continent. Only two years before the Erie Canal had been opened between Albany and the Great Lakes; hundreds of thousands of immigrants and Americans were on the move.

So when his boss made him his offer, the spirit of independence re-awoke in Cornelius. He turned the offer down. Not with grateful thanks: as soon appeared, he had a 'smarter' idea. One new thing he had learned on the river was the beauty of rate-cutting. Corneel let his boss sell to a new owner and then, having bought an old boat or two on the side, he ran them in competition at ruinous rates, until the new owner was soon forced to buy him off. This ploy became an important and life-long practice in his rise as a carrier. He put the money into new or patched up

William Henry Vanderbilt's mansion at 640 Fifth Avenue, New York – a vast rococo brownstone with 58 rooms; sixt

sculptors were engaged to decorate it. In the 1890s Vanderbilt houses dominated Fifth Avenue from 51st to 58th Streets.

ships and left the river for the coastwise trade on Long Island and up the coast of Connecticut while still keeping in with Albany. And with this he pulled his unhappy family out of New Brunswick and put them into a mean house in New York. While he skimped on ships, wife and children, the money rolled in. It was impossible for a spry man to fail: New York, now with a population of 100,000, was a fare collector's, a map-filler's paradise; when one of the chronic outbreaks of cholera came, Corneel did handsomely out of getting the frightened inhabitants out to healthy Connecticut.

New York wealth was still in the hands of the old stock who lived in style and kept newcomers out, except the Astors who had cunningly exploited the new grid-like plan of the city. They had bought up the convenient lots of standard 25-foot frontage and pocketed the rents as the city grew. Cornelius could not compete with this yet, but he formalised his appearance and if he scorned the Society that would have nothing to do with him, he was distinctive. The rough sailor was now disguised in a uniform that he never afterwards changed. He appeared in a long frock coat, a high collar with a flourishing cravat, wore a top hat, always had a cigar in his mouth and carried the well-known cane. Without the beard, he was Uncle Sam to the life. His language had not changed; and if, like many self-driving Americans, he was tortured by a bad stomach, this itself seemed rather to whip up his energy, his caustic tongue and blunt decisions. It was a waste of money to put lifebelts on his ships; a waste of money to insure them. Better to keep every penny for new vessels.

It is truly said that America enlarges the ego at the expense of any other aspects of the personality. As a self-made man he had turned into a ruthless egotist. He liked enemies, but at home he seems to have treated his wife and children as no more than aggravations. They disappointed him. At 40 he was very much the American mother's boy, emotionally underdeveloped and entirely self-willed. If he hoped his wife would get the family into Society, she cowered and did not even try. She feared and hated New York and wept at her lot. She was still the poor girl from Staten Island. Their daughters had been given a little education, but they were no more than strapping. One by one they married and that was the end of them as far as their father was concerned. The two sons were impossible. The elder, William Henry, had not the slightest interest in his father's business: he had been sent to a grammar school but his only talent was for miserable accountancy and, whatever went on secretly in his life, he was servile and obsequious with his hot-tempered father who had nothing but contempt for him when the lad took to piety and married the daughter of an obscure minister. Cornelius refused to give him a penny. William Henry failed as a clerk and the only thing to do with him was to make him a small farmer. The second son, Cornelius Jeremiah, was a disaster and here the father was plagued by guilt for he saw himself being punished for marrying a first cousin: the youth was an epileptic, a drunkard, a liar and the creepy black sheep who ran up gambling debts in his father's name and was in and out of the flourishing brothels of the city. The only other boy was adored, but he was a child still.

By now the railway age had begun and, as at the time of the first steamers, the Commodore – so people called him – would have nothing to do with the new thing. He took one trip in a train and was very nearly killed in a bad accident; the early railways were dangerous. His enormous strength pulled him through, but he came out of it with a strained heart. He softened to the extent of deciding to settle with his family on Staten Island and built himself a bizarre Gothic house which was fronted by marble pillars: he had just reached the million mark and from his porch could survey the flags of his fleet and commute to New York by the ferry he owned. There's a story that he was once a little late for it and that the Captain refused to return a few yards for him. The Commodore gave a nod of approval. He liked an employee who kept to schedule, even at the expense of the boss. The incident brought two wrongs to his mind. First, his silly wife had cost him a big house whereas his proud mother refused to move from her old cottage. Secondly, he was bored. He ought never to have softened. The old Cornelius was reborn: he went over to New York and without telling his wife started building a large gloomy house on Washington Square: he was going to force her into Society. The poor woman had reached the menopause and became frantic. She refused to go. The Commodore was not going to stand that. He sent her off to Canada and when that didn't "cure" her he decided she was mad and had her put into what was virtually an asylum. To his astonishment, the whole family, including his mother, turned on him. The obscure William Henry led the attack and said plainly that the cause of the trouble was his father's love affair with a housekeeper. He told his father that the scandal would ruin his business. Only at this did the Commodore give in. The gloomy house was finished, Sophia returned and he agreed at any rate to give public consideration to the wife who bored him.

He went back to the infighting of the trade and his rate cutting campaigns. He got over his hatred of

THE GREAT RACE FOR THE WESTERN STAKES 1870

Only late in life did the Commodore lose his scorn of the railroads. When he did enter the race, he was unstoppable.

railways, for he saw the profit in connecting his ships with the small railways that were running to the Connecticut ports. America gave him another big helping hand: steamers had run on wood, now coal from Pennsylvania was coming in, dug out by cheap immigrant labour. In these years, he was sometimes in partnership with a pious rogue called Daniel Drew who is important because he marks the difference between the Commodore and the main crowd who were in the money game, where 'out-smarting' had become a kind of ethic, rather like art for art's sake on a low level. The difference is that the Commodore believed in power, selfish though it was, in building an empire and linking the transport systems that were opening up the country. He was long-headed, whereas Drew was the speculator, going for the quick shady gamble, without any end but the instant coup. Drew is said to be responsible for the well-known Wall Street words "stock-watering". When he was a poor young man Drew had diddled one of the Astors by driving a herd of scrawny cattle to a riverside place outside New York

and, before the sale, he filled them up with salt. The thirsty cattle swelled up to prize dimensions when they drank and Astor paid a high price for what was really gallons of water. The 'con-man' has a respectable place in American folklore from Mark Twain to Perelman and was the sort of man Vanderbilt loved to outwit the richer he became.

But once more, when one considers the dirty and half-savage tricks of the American free-for-all at this time, the hero is the American soil. In 1848, the year of crushed revolutions in Europe, when millions of defeated workers got away to America, gold was discovered in California. An orgy had begun, an orgy that would last a decade and would transform the country. Gold would free the United States from foreign bankers and ease the strain under which a recklessly expanded economy suffered. The shipping and foreign trade would be doubled. A loosely organised country of little townships and scattered cities would become a Great Power at last. Although they were swindled by shippers who brought them, 41 although they were the prey of the dock-side, the carriers and the lodging houses, the immigrants arrived in their tens of thousands, with Balzacian dreams in their heads.

The Commodore was not the man to join an orgy and get out quickly with a sudden profit. He was a slow thinker, a man looking for the key to the situation. He knew there was no railway across the country. He noted that in one year 750 ships had left New York for San Francisco. He noted that they sailed to Panama, transhipped by rail across the isthmus and were picked up by ships on the Pacific side. The snag was that the Line that carried the bulk of the passengers, held an exclusive government licence for mail and cargo and charged 500 dollars the trip.

A monopoly! The spirit of his rate-cutting piracy on the Hudson River monopoly suddenly awoke in the Commodore. If he had no clear dramatic vision, he had an eye for detail and for knowing how to pick the lock of a door that was closed to him. Always a man for maps, he got out his map of Central America and studied it. He noted there was no need to go to Panama. He could cut out the monopoly if he could get across Nicaragua. There was an immense lake in the middle of the country. If you could get to it you could land passengers within eleven miles of the Pacific, cut the journey by 500 miles and a week off the time, on condition that you could get a steamer up the river from San Juan del Norte on the Atlantic side. The prospect had the excitement of a steamboat race and a battle combined. There were three difficulties. The first was political, but that was nothing: in those days one didn't pay taxes, one bought politicians and dished them later. The second was to get ships over the rapids and rocks of the long swift river to the lake. The third was to get through the mountains on the Pacific side. With a fierce leap of imagination – uncommon with him – the Commodore took the greatest difficulty first: he would raise a huge loan and cut a canal eleven miles long through the mountains. The idea was preposterous: time and cost made it impossible, though he did try Barings in London and failed. The fact is that he didn't seriously think he would get the canal. It was essentially a bluff and a fantasy, no more than bait for investors in Nicaragua and America who would believe they might have Barings's money behind them. He formed the Accessory Transit Company: the investors rushed to it. Then the Commodore became an Imperialist. He tackled the politicians in Nicaragua and persuaded them to stage a *coup d'état* by promising them a laughable 10,000 dollars on signing the contract for building the canal: he gave them 200,000 dollars in stock and twenty per cent of the profits for twenty years for exclusive rights to the route. The value of the shares shot up. When he announced that the British had turned down the scheme and the shares fell, Vanderbilt bought them at par and pocketed the profit, a classic piece of stock-watering in the best Daniel Drew tradition. But this was only the first move. Accessory Transit did not give up their route. The Commodore had not been a rough river captain for nothing. He was determined to get a ship up the impossible river. He steamed to Nicaragua in one of his small ships, *The Director*, to force it up the river from the Caribbean port. The Nicaraguans, for whom he had contempt, warned him of rapids and rocks, so he took command himself, roaring that he would make the ship jump the rocks under full steam with safety valve tied down in the old Hudson River style. And he *did* make *The Director* jump them or, when he couldn't, he plumbed the channels and either warped the ship up by cables tied to the trees on the bank or dynamited the obstructions. His bad heart got better: at fifty-four he had recovered his youth.

This river journey was the hellish part of the voyage which was eventually endured by 2000 passengers a month in the next nine years. He put a fleet of his worst patched-up ships on the route – if he knew how to build a fine ship or two he was a notorious patcher-up of old stock – and the journey was a scandalous package of overcrowding, bad food, accident and robbery. The skippers were rough-necks and incompetent. As they said, you didn't bottlefeed people who had the gold fever. If passengers claimed for injury or death, they got nothing. One of his ships, *The Independent*, which met passengers on the Pacific side, hit a reef. Its boiler burst, the ship caught fire and 150 people drowned for his ships never had enough life boats and he still refused to insure them – waste of money. The company, he said, was not responsible for human error or acts of God: the journey was a package, take it or leave it. There was one reward for those who survived the river. The lake was peaceful and smart coaches painted blue and white, the Nicaraguan colours, took them over mountain roads only a little less awful than the river, to the Pacific port. The Panama Monopoly was enraged when the Commodore cut his fares from 500 dollars first class to 300 and steerage from 125 to 35. Eventually he got the fare from New York to San Francisco down to 50 dollars.

A share speculator like Drew would have cleared a quick profit and sold out long before. Not so Vanderbilt. He saw he had years of power and profit ahead of him. Having got the Accessory Transit Company established, the Commodore built himself one of the

The North Star, **the first of Cornelius Vanderbilt's luxury steam yachts; the dining saloon was walled in with marble.**

first of his luxurious ocean-going yachts, *The North Star.* He was going to sail to Britain and astonish Europe. He could afford it, he said: he had 11 millions invested and at 25 per cent he had an annual income of nearly 3 million, tax free. *The North Star* was 270 feet long with a 38-foot beam; its dining saloon was walled in with yellow Pyrenean marble with panels of Naples granite. Its ceiling was white with scrolls of purple, green and gold. His mother who was 80 was too old to go with him. She waved from Staten Island as *The North Star* passed to the Narrows. All his family, except Cornelius Jeremiah, the black sheep, were on board. They sailed to England where the Press called him a new Cosimo de Medici sprung to life, but fashionable London society snubbed the millionaire and his family. They even found it hard to get into an hotel. Their hopes of meeting the Queen and Prince Albert did not come off but they were entertained at the Mansion House and the public cheered the American wonder. The next stop was St Petersburg and there society was delighted with them. The Czar loaned one of the Imperial carriages to the Commodore and his wife.

But the Nicaraguan story was not ended and indeed became ugly. He had left his Line, the Accessory Transit, in the hands of partners Morgan and Garrison. Immediately after he left for Europe they plotted to rob him of his company. They employed a filibuster called Walker to get political control of Nicaragua by a *coup d'état* of their own. Walker landed with guns, threw out the government and got the new government to cancel Vanderbilt's franchise and take his ships. He heard the black news when he got back to New York and at once he wrote the rogues a famous letter. He liked a fight in the open but they had stabbed him in the back. He was out for a revenge that would drive them out of the trade altogether. He wrote: "Gentlemen: You have undertaken to cheat me. I will not sue you because the law takes too long. I will ruin you."

His mother had died while he was away and it is thought that grief added ferocity to his plans. To begin with he started a new Company, The People's Independent Line – and, since they had stolen his Nicaraguan franchise, he threatened to run it to Panama which was not his territory and cut the rates to a quarter. The partners were scared and tried to buy him off by giving him 400,000 for *The North Star* and gave him back control. They offered him 670,000 dollars to keep out and he took it. But he had promised ruin and he did not rest until he had knocked the rogues out of shipping for good. They fought back for a while. Their man Walker had done as he had promised. He had gone to Nicaragua with fifty men and thrown out the President and taken over Vanderbilt's ships: but Vanderbilt stopped sailings on both sides of the country and bottled up Walker in the country. "One more

43

fight", Howden Smith, a biographer who has caught the Commodore's language, reports him as saying was "no mor'n mustard on my ham". He persuaded the governments of Honduras, Guatemala, San Salvador and Costa Rica to throw out Walker's President and Walker had to surrender to the American navy. Having savagely defeated the plot, having "made his p'int" and got the utmost out of his robbers, he astonished them by dropping out of the Nicaraguan business altogether. He had perceived what no-one else had: that the Gold Rush was coming to an end. The real sufferers were the Nicaraguans but he cared nothing about that. Their country returned to anarchy and misery. More than any other American act this one established Latin America's lasting hatred of American financial imperialism.

After Nicaragua, a piece of low comedy enlivens his private story. He was in his sixties, still strong but made irascible by dyspepsia, kidney trouble and a bad heart. It is no surprise, considering the reckless way he treated his body, that he could not sleep at night and he was driven to fury by New York's squalling cats. He hit on the idea of getting a lad known as Ikey Vesuvius from one of the street gangs and offering him a dollar for every dead cat he could bring in. This budding millionaire and his friends brought in a hundred from all over the city. The Commodore was not going to be tricked like that and refused to pay: so the boys picked up all the cats they could find, tied their tails and threw them over the wall into his garden. He paid up. What was keeping him awake was the fight to create a shipping empire in the Atlantic.

But in 1861 – he was 67 now – the Civil War came. He had never shown any interest in politics or political ideas, but he came out on Lincoln's side simply because his expanding trade had played an important part in drawing the whole country together. His patriotic instinct was for unity. (There was a private reason also: his favourite and youngest son had been allowed to go to West Point. The father would have stopped the older sons but this boy was allowed to do as he pleased. Tragically, he died of fever in hospital.)

44 **Railroads and shipping – the transport tycoons of the Eighties, with William H. Vanderbilt at their head.**

The Commodore lent his fleet and best ship, *The Vanderbilt*, to the Union army – there was a row afterwards about the money he made. What four years of war brought home to him was the importance of the detestable railways: only the railways could follow the armies in the field and reach the once empty interior of the country. When peace came, the soldiers returning home would become passengers and buyers who would demand train loads of goods. Despite his suspicions of the railways and his scorn for the railway boom which had created a number of small weak companies with ill-laid tracks, he had cunningly bought up here and there, just as he had bought up second-hand ships. He began now to put his war profits into the little New York Central that ran from Harlem to Albany and Buffalo – a key fragment in the direct route to the Great Lakes.

By the time he was in his seventies the battle for empire went to Wall Street and he was soon in the thick of the biggest fight of his life with speculators like slimy old Drew. Fisk, Gould and Boss Tweed, the most notorious rascals New York had yet known, were key figures in the financial scramble. Tweed, the Scottish bribery king, was the Vanderbilt agent in Albany. The mad railway boom was an affair of writs, lawsuits, of buying and selling judges, of stock-watering, even the printing of false share certificates, flights beyond the jurisdiction of the State courts. Tweed eventually went to prison and Fisk was shot dead by the time the boom was over and famous Wall Street firms ruined in the appalling slump which taught the public they had been robbed. But the end of it all was that Vanderbilt came out of it on top, with an empire complete and his railway running for the first time for thirty years into Grand Central, the heart of New York. His fortune had jumped up to seventy million.

How to account for the old man's burst of youthful vigour which raged on until he was eighty-three? He was one of those who kept their youth. Power was his passion; he had no use for splendour. He worked in a bare little office which contained only a small table and a chair. The office was at the back of his house. He held his business in his head, stuck a note or two on some matter in the table drawer and kept his mouth shut about what he was doing. He amused himself still with his trotters, puffed his cigars – never offered one to anyone else – and played whist. He had one secret misery: the dissipations of his black sheep son. Then his wife died and he was surprised by grief, repentance and loneliness.

His inner life took a bizarre turn: he took to investing in spiritualism and the world beyond the grave

William Henry Vanderbilt – "The public be damned"

and his share-holding took an erotic direction. Instead of housemaids and the ladies he met at the trotting races, female mediums and spiritualists, magnetic healers, expert in the laying on of hands, became his taste. As they consoled, they put him in touch with the dead, particularly with his mother and with the wife he had neglected. His sexual life started to resemble that of Balzac's Baron Nucingen, the senile banker: a sordid yet refreshing spell of erotic farce entered the Commodore's life in his friendship with the notorious Victoria Woodhull and Tennessee Claflin, a business-like pair of young women from Ohio who went in for the occult and who publicly wrote of free love, feminism and socialism. If his interest was romantic, it had its incurable business side: he set the two women up as stockbrokers and with his help they did well. He even wanted to marry Tennessee. The family were horrified but the Commodore kept to the instincts of a lifetime: even as he was courting Tennessee he was falling for a Southern girl fifty years younger than himself and who was, in a distant way, a relative: the Commodore had always 45 preferred to work within the family. She was the grand-daughter of his mother's brother who had disappeared in her childhood. The young woman had to be divorced first before she could get the Commodore, but she was determined and they were married at last. In a panic the aging Vanderbilt daughters, one or two of them widows, wasted their time trying to nag the Commodore into dividing his fortune equally among them. They loathed the young wife: her name was Frank. One can imagine the sneers. But no-one had ever been able to frustrate the Commodore's intentions at any time in his life, except perhaps his mother. Frank certainly was after money, but she transformed him. He stopped swearing, he improved his grammar: she turned the spiritualists out, led him to religion or, at any rate, got him to read Bunyan's *Pilgrim's Progress*. The self-applauding Bunyan had more than once consoled the guilty capitalists of the past and would console many to come. They had met many of Bunyan's worldly wisemen in business. The Commodore had never been a philanthropist and he mistrusted education: his second wife's most remarkable act was to get him to found Vanderbilt

William Kissam Vanderbilt I and (opposite) his socially ambitious wife Alva, in elaborate costume for a ball.

University, and act clean against his nature.

In 1877, at the age of eighty-three, the Commodore died. He died in agony. Every organ of the powerful body that had ferried his periaugers across New York harbour when the city was no more than a little Dutch town had rotted away. The family, New York, Wall Street above all, waited to hear his will. Would the estate be equally divided? Cornelius Jeremiah, the epileptic sinner who had pledged his father's name so often, was the most eager to know. With growing indignation the family heard that although there were adequate bequests to all, the huge bulk of the fortune was to go to William Henry. Cornelius Jeremiah was not disinherited but his small share was put outside his control.

There was war at once, Cornelius Jeremiah leading the attack. The old man was insane, they said. The female mediums and his new wife had played on a senile mind. America has always had more lawyers to the square mile than any other country in the world. Nothing is more sacred than the right of every citizen to sue for a million dollars. And it was exceptional in these money-mad years for a will *not* to be contested. So New York was diverted by one of the most squalid will disputes of its history. Seventy million was the prize. Unforgettable figures of sleazy American life came to court. Detectives, real or bogus, were tracking Cornelius Jeremiah to brothels; prostitutes and racketeers came up from the country; the mediums, crystal gazers, even a phrenologist, were called. The astute ladies, Victoria Woodhull and Tennessee Claflin, suddenly disappeared to Europe with a good deal of money to carry on their magnetic art and preaching. But the Commodore was declared sane, the will stood though the heir eased it by minor compromises. One or two of the lawyers made enough money to retire from the Bar for good. Cornelius Jeremiah ran through his extra cash in a few years and then shot himself.

The Commodore was one of those who want to rule from beyond the grave. His will was designed to preserve the name of Vanderbilt and to keep the empire within the family; to do that he had put the bulk of the fortune into the one competent and above all obedient pair of hands. Over fifty years old, obese, unhealthy though he was and kept under his father's thumb, William Henry was just the man, the man of respectable talent, to consolidate what genius had created. The Commodore had noted years before that the prosaic farmer-accountant had done modestly well on Staten Island. He admired the way his son had dished him over a ferry-load of manure and had spotted William Henry's gifts in the railway business

when he skilfully revived a little railway only thirteen miles long on the island. Cautiously the Commodore had gradually given him jobs at the Grand Central office. The son revealed that he was a secretive but reliable speculator: he revered profit. And he loved trotters.

William Henry, the new King of Grand Central, at once set about finding a new father-figure: the banker Pierpont Morgan and he moved a large share of his capital into investments. America itself expanded them for him and doubled his fortune to the tune of 200 million before he died. He skilfully survived the dramatic slumps and panics; was brutal in the inevitable strikes – he called in the militia – although he denied saying it, the newspapers swore he uttered, in one crisis, the damning phrase "The public be damned". The fact is that the Vanderbilts were so rich that it was impossible for the wildest expenditure to catch up with their mortally increasing income.

This had been noticed by the new generation of Vanderbilt women. Indeed American women in general, whether their husbands were successful or not, lived in a state of domestic prudery and latent rapacity. The Commodore's mother had been content to preserve her independence and live modestly in Staten Island, his wife had been an acquiescent chattel. William Henry's wife remained comfortably domestic and saw her children were well-educated. It rankled less with her than with her sons, and above all their wives, that they were not admitted to the fashionable society, based on old wealth, ruled by the power of Mrs Astor in her mansion at 39th Street which in the Seventies was the limit of New York's notion of a good address. The new Vanderbilt women wanted "a slice of the action", an enormous slice of social dominance.

The stifled passion of the women had deep roots in the history of New York itself. As the chief gate to the country New York was closer to European luxury than any other city. The age of the Titanesses had arrived. In that polished if searing classic of American morals in the 19th century, *The Mauve Decade*, Thomas Beer quotes a neurologist saying to a male patient that his meaningless deference to the wishes of Mrs X has "caused her to tear down a superb Georgian house while the husband was abroad and to order the creation of a French *manoir* in white stone which hideously existed until it happened to burn ten years later." And went on to say that the Titanesses swarmed all over Europe, acquiring stereotyped clothes, furniture, attention and parasites with "that wide-eyed credulity which remain their excuse and charm".

Not the style of the Vanderbilt women or the taste

'Alice of the Breakers' – Mrs Cornelius Vanderbilt II and (opposite) her husband, the Commodore's grandson.

of their men who had most of them been sent to Europe for their education; but it evokes scenes which enabled Henry James to write *Daisy Miller* and some of his comments on Americans abroad. New York had always the first helpings of European luxury. It had always gone in for banquets, balls, big houses, luxurious clothes; it had always gone in for expense, despite its pretensions to Victorian decorum which was the one powerful weapon the women had in wars with their money-making men. *Their* status was now not in Wall Street alone, but in what they could unload in jewellery, clothes, and mansions on the women. The women's demands became far greater: they wanted the loot of Europe. They wanted palaces, châteaux like Fontainebleau or Blois or Italian palazzos and everything inside them, all the statues, all the pictures, all the flunkeys. Why not? By the Nineties, in a mere 100 years, New York had grown from a little Dutch town of 20,000 people, into a metropolis of a million and a half.

The first step in creating a fashionable society is to build an opera house. New York had long ago built 49

MRS. CORNELIUS VANDERBILT

one, called the Academy of Music; and the old families had soon arranged matters so that the parvenus like the Vanderbilts were kept out. William Henry offered 30,000 dollars for the season and was turned down. So he got a group of the insulted to build a larger one which cost at least a million. They established what was called the Diamond Circle for their families. There in boxes which were sometimes festooned with orchids, the new rich displayed themselves and were anxious that their jewels should be seen. One Vanderbilt lady went to her seat with a rope of pearls tied to her waist, at the end of which a huge sapphire hung which she kicked along as she walked. Another had her chair raised so that the value of her loaded bosom could be estimated. The fashion for obelisks, created as long ago as Napoleon's day, was still alive: William Henry paid for the importation of an obelisk. Philanthropy was no certain road to social éclat, but art was. And if Americans of this time were mocked for their ingenuous greed for solid chunks of tangible culture, the middle classes in Europe had been quietly doing the same thing, but over a longer period.

The first of the Vanderbilt women to get off the mark was Alva, the wife of William Henry's second surviving son, William Kissam Vanderbilt, known in the annals as Willie K, who had worked his way up in the business. He had been educated in Europe. Alva was the daughter of a Southern cotton merchant from one of the richest families of the South, but the Civil War had ruined him. This did not dismay Alva's mother, who, with the American talent for rising briskly from disaster, opened a boarding house in New York. One of Alva's closest friends had married the Duke of Manchester; her sister had married the bride's brother. Alva was virtually a socialite. She was a pretty if plump young woman, rather heavy in the chin and was determined to force Mrs Astor to accept the Vanderbilts. She soon persuaded Willie K to spend three million on a palace at 52nd street and Fifth Avenue which, at that time, was almost country and well to the north of fashion. The architect constructed a mixture of the Château de Blois and a Renaissance mansion put up by a 15th-century financier at Bourges. It was built in Caen stone imported from France and was decorated in Regency style, complete with stained glass, tapestries and banqueting hall. Alva gave a spectacular ball to which the Astors and their daughter were not invited. They had not, Alva pointed out, 'called'. For her daughter's sake, Mrs Astor gave in. It was a costume ball, intended to rival the balls of Versailles. Willie K was dressed as the Duc de Guise, his wife was a Venetian princess. His elder brother Cornelius was Louis XVI

Consuelo, Willie K.'s daughter, who married the Duke of Marlborough. Opposite: Grace, wife of Cornelius III.

and his wife came as an electric light. When the Hobby Horse Quadrille began the ladies wore red coats and the gentlemen red coats and satin knee breeches and danced inside artificial horses made of real horse hide. It was the most splendid ball New York had ever known and had cost 75,000 dollars plus the enormous sums paid for the costumes.

His son's mansion put William Henry on his mettle and he built a palace of his own and outdid his son. Between 51st and 52nd street he built an enormous rococo brownstone with fifty-eight rooms. He brought in sixty sculptors and carvers to decorate it. The great bronze entrance doors had been bought from an Italian prince; the floors were of North African marble and in the vestibule stood a great vase of malachite, eight feet high – its fellow was in the Czar's palace at St Petersburg. The marble columns of the central hall rose four storeys to the roof, with balconies on every floor in the Italian manner, and every inch was stuffed 51

Opposite: Willie K. II, the motor-racing and yachting enthusiast, and (above) Virginia Graham Fair, his first wife.

with bronzes and statuary. On one wall was a tapestry of Agamemnon and Iphigenia, on the ceiling was a medieval hunting scene. Some of the statues were dramatic: one at the foot of the staircase was a life-size gilded slave girl with one breast exposed. She wore a tiara that lit up at night. Inside a palace in which the exhibits stood jumbled side by side, William Henry displayed his particular interest: his large collection of academic pictures. They were jammed, in all shapes and sizes, as in a sales room. He had little taste; but having been a farmer for years before he was a railway magnate, he had a touching interest in landscapes and farmyard pictures of the traditional kind. He travelled once a year to France and Italy in search of them. (The richest man in the world was often seen in Paris carrying a brown paper parcel containing his boots to be repaired.) He loved showing his collection to the public. There was a curious hunger for the arts in this florid and deeply retentive man who ate too much and had high blood pressure.

Other Vanderbilts joined the spree of building ostentatious mansions in Fifth Avenue. There was soon a colony of them more or less next door to one another. The ladies spent millions on decorations and specialised in New York's taste for banquets and balls which grew more fantastic as the Gilded Age came in.

The Vanderbilt males traipsed after their wives who were pursuing European titles and royalty and out-doing Mrs Astor. But she beat them all: the Astors left the country and got a title of their own. It rankled. The parties became more idiotic. Here Mrs Fish, a cynical heiress, triumphed: her speciality was making fools of her guests. At one of her parties a baby elephant went round offering peanuts; at another boys dressed up as cats, handed out the favours to the ladies; the favours were white mice. There was a dinner party for dolls and the guests were made to use baby talk at dinner. There was a banquet for dogs at which the dog guests wore diamond collars costing 15,000 dollars – all material for Veblen's famous book on the American ideal of Conspicuous Waste.

But not all the Vanderbilts wanted to build on Fifth Avenue. One interesting exception was William Henry's youngest son, George Washington Vanderbilt II. A crankish solitary, his notion was to create not an empire but a medieval domain and the biggest palace in the continent. He moved south and bought 100,000 acres of forest in North Carolina, built himself a far grander Château de Blois than anyone else's with the largest roof in America and a Norman banqueting hall seventy feet high. The place had forty bedrooms. He was trying to create a benevolent feudal community   53 with its own village, shops and schools and roads and he employed 750 people, the poor white of that region – cheap labour again. There he landscaped, and bred cattle. He was a first-rate linguist. Alas this talent was put to the futile task of translating modern works into ancient Greek; still, his knowledge of forestry was of lasting benefit to the American government. But the ennui and the restlessness of the rich afflicted him in the end: he gave up his feudal kingdom, went tiger shooting in India and eventually married a very rich woman and settled prosaically in Washington.

In 1885 the cautious William Henry died. He left 200 million and for a day or two the frightened stock-markets of the world closed and waited to hear his will. When it was read the public saw that one more Vanderbilt had disobeyed his father: he had split up his fortune, though he put control of the railroad into the hands of his two sons: another Cornelius, the only philanthropist of the family – very admired by the public – and Willie K, the yachtsman and polo player. The two wives quarrelled bitterly but the brothers got on well and for a time it did not seem that the split in control of the empire mattered. There were no death duties, income tax was trivial and, indeed, railway earnings were exempt.

* * * * *

New York summers are hard to endure. The old Commodore used to retire to Saratoga Springs, but the new generations went to Newport on Rhode Island and built summer 'cottages' there. Willie K spent eleven million on the Marble House for his wife; her rival, Alice, to whom she did not speak, replied with an enormous Italian palazzo – but with an extra floor on top for her servants – called The Breakers. Huge chunks of Italian art were brought over; inside, it was a grotesque museum of marble, alabaster and gilt-and-gingerbread fantasies. Alice gave dinners for 200 guests who arrived in carriages with their valets and ladies' maids, kept thirty-three servants and sixteen footmen dressed in wigs and maroon silk breeches. Alva, the careless masterful Southern charm-er next door fought back: the title of 'The Mrs Vanderbilt' was the prize and Alva had nerve. She did the un-speakable. Willie K was bored with her; she got herself divorced from him and married a multi-millionaire banker without losing a jot of her power and fame as a hostess. Better still, a few years later, she gave an even more enormous ball than usual, broke off her daughter Consuelo's engagement and with some violence forced her to marry the Duke of Marlborough. A Duke for the Vanderbilts; a Vanderbilt at Blenheim where money was short!

54 **The Breakers – Alice Vanderbilt's vast 'summer cottage' at Newport, Rhode Island.**

And this was not the end of the battle of Newport. Alice and her husband had to withstand a private blow. Their eldest son had died at Yale while still an undergraduate. The heir was now Neily, a shy and studious young man who disliked society and whose interests were entirely in science, engineering and invention. He suffered from chronic rheumatism. He fell in love with a pretty Southerner, Grace Wilson, a few years older than himself, and she with him, and once more the classic Vanderbilt struggle between father and son began. The father said the boy was too young: he had not seen the world, whereas the delightful girl had seen too much of it. She had been brought up in Europe, had been engaged already a couple of times and had moved in a 'fast set' of royalty and nobility. The Prince of Wales thought her a "pet". She was well off. Perhaps Neily's father had the sort of objection a rich man of the third generation would have for the wealth of a self-made man. The wealth of Grace Wilson's father was suspect in Northern eyes. The son of a poor Scottish tanner, he had started as a pedlar – as, indeed, the original Astor had done. He had been a smart salesman, who had charmed cotton out of unworldly small growers in the South during the Civil War and had made a fortune for them in London – a treachery from the Union point of view. He was a genial original, totally without the Vanderbilt stubbornness and he glided easily in European and American society. Whatever the reasons for Cornelius's objections, Neily fought his father with all the Vanderbilt pride and temper – short temper was the trait that seems to have been handed down from the Commodore – and the couple married against the father's command. The father refused to see him again.

In fact the father, the evangelical Cornelius II, was right. Embittered by his father's reaction, Neily became a lonely figure, married to a ravishing girl whose taste was for theatrical splash and the limelight. Grace Vanderbilt became the most famous of the Vanderbilt hostesses. By a lucky twist of fate she became mistress of 640 Fifth Avenue; a posthumous revenge on the father-in-law who had hated her, for she had split the family into two factions in a long-lasting feud. She was the Queen of New York, the slender, glamorous enchantress who poured her money away. Her crowd of footmen and servants were sent up and down between New York and Newport: even the top servants were looted from Europe. With them went the Gobelins tapestry before which she sat enthroned. She outbid her rivals by getting the brother of the Kaiser to one of her dinners. She entertained eventually all the royalty of Europe. The tragedy was that Neily hated the whole thing. He had been shut out of the family business though he was allowed to invent a new locomotive. He had his yachts on which he began to drink heavily. He got something out of being an officer in the Militia, saw a touch of action in the Mexican war and in 1917 went to France for a short time as a General. And, in due time, he quarrelled with *his* son who turned gossip writer.

640 Fifth Avenue was the last of the Vanderbilt mansions in New York. When Grace Vanderbilt died the famous malachite vase went to the Metropolitan. Slowly the control of the huge railway system which had spread a web over America fell out of the family's hands into the hands of bankers. As a family, the carriers became rich and restless passengers. They passed their time as sportsmen and travellers, and playboys in the cosmopolitan world of Edwardian luxury, often charming, sometimes impossible, but leaving no mark. They were too instant. Wealthier than the old European aristocracies, they had not the ingrained staying power of landowners, and nothing like the same sense of traditional responsibility or serviceable legend. It is true that they have left a University and one or two interesting minor museums. They were collectors. They produced no statesmen and no eccentrics and any minor gifts they had seem to have led them into gentlemanly amateurism. Their will died of nothing to bite on. The Commodore is the only powerful figure among them. Willie K, who consoled himself after Alva divorced him by going to live in France and looking after his racing stables, summed up what had eaten into the will of the Commodore's descendants. Willie K had worked hard in the railway office for periods, but he had tired of that and amused himself, either intelligently or rashly. He had become a spectator of himself. He said at the end of his life:

> My life was never destined to be quite happy. It was laid out along lines which I could foresee almost from my earliest childhood. It has left me with nothing to hope for, with nothing definite to seek or strive for. Inherited wealth is a real handicap to happiness. It is as certain as death to ambition as cocaine is to morality. If a man makes money, no matter how much, he finds a certain happiness in its possession, for in the desire to increase his business he has a constant use for it. The first satisfaction and the greatest, that of building the foundation of a fortune, is denied him. He must labour, if he does labour, simply to add to an over-sufficiency.

By the fourth generation the vivid splash of the Vanderbilts was over. Even their monument – Grand Central Station – belonged no more to them.

The railway age: in popular myth it was glamour and adventure; to the Vanderbilts it was a triumph.

The railway age: the work force was cheap and plentiful; the Vanderbilt fortunes multiplied.

FORD

David Caute

Opposite: Henry Ford photographed in 1865. He was two-and-a-half.

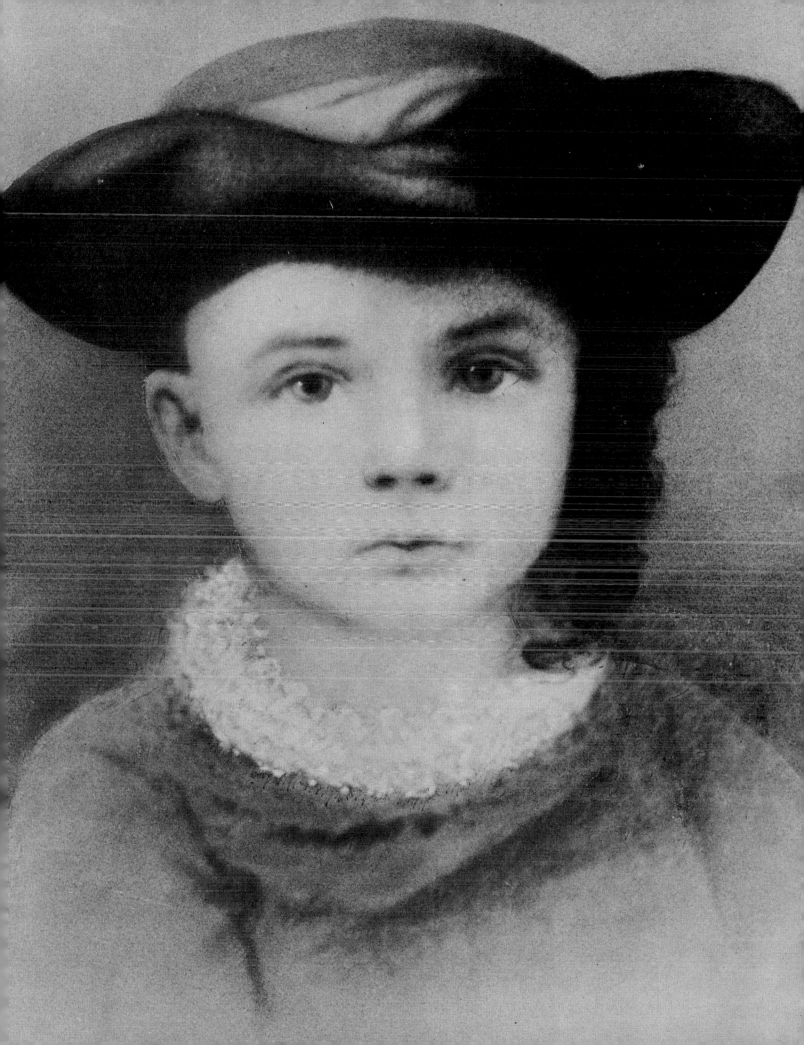

Henry Ford (top row, third from right) in 1893, then an engineer at the Edison Illuminating Company. Overleaf: *Det*

dustry, **by the Mexican Marxist artist Diego Rivera, commissioned by Edsel Ford in 1932 for the Detroit Institute of Arts.**

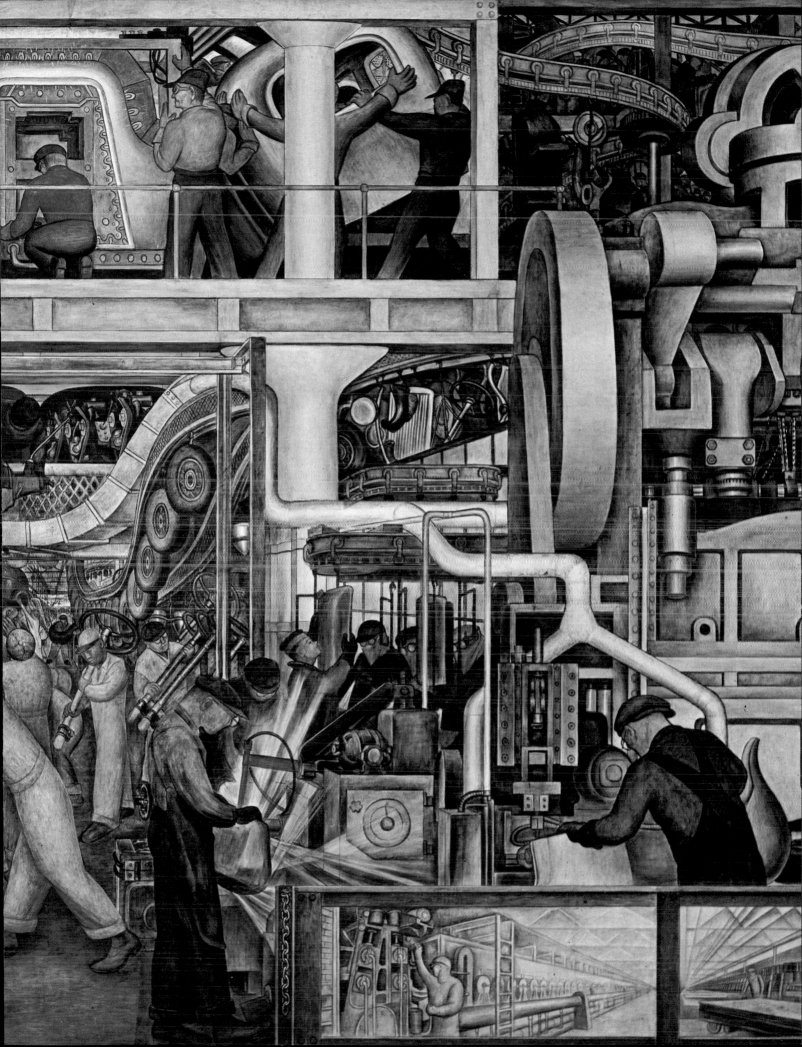

The homestead at Dearborn, Michigan, where Henry Ford was born in 1863.

"They say," my chauffeur remarked softly, gliding the big, 9000-dollar Lincoln 'Town Car' down the Edsel Ford Freeway, "that Mr Ford was very fond of nature."

"The first Mr Ford?"

"Yes sir. You know, one of my buddies used to drive for Mr Ford. Mr Ford would tell my buddy, 'Stop here,' and then Mr Ford would jump out, you know, leap over the fence, a couple of handsprings maybe, and sprint across the field and lie under a tree for an hour, sometimes two."

"Asleep?"

"That I can't say, sir. And then one day, you know, he came home and found this robin nesting above his door and he had the door nailed up so she could raise her family. Mr Ford was very fond of nature."

"I don't supose that the present Mr Ford has time to do that."

The chauffeur smiled uneasily. With unemployment at over twenty per cent, wariness pervades the deferential hush of the Dearborn monarchy; Ford World Headquarters, from the lavish vice-presidential 11th floor down to the chauffeurs and mechanics in the basement garages, is a syndrome of discretion dominated by the latest utterance of the man on the 12th floor. The man, as American reporters like to put it, with his name over the door.

Travelling smoothly across the grey-green flatland of Michigan, the vast industrial estate which extends north-east to the Great Lakes, the visitor may well reflect that building long, swollen automobiles which gulp a gallon of gasoline every fourteen miles is no longer a very exciting, or a very social, thing to do. But there was a time, sixty, seventy years ago, when Edison, Ford, Duryea, Durant, Leland and the Wright brothers were pioneering a new industrial age, the age which carried America into the American Century, when the mass production of a strong, light, durable and above all cheap motor car transformed the economic life and geographical horizons of a whole continent. This is what Henry Ford did, and millions of Americans admired his achievement.

And yet the prospects for the Ford Motor Company when it was incorporated in 1903 were hardly auspicious. Although Ford had made his name with racing cars (in 1904 he personally beat the world speed record on the ice of the St Clair River, recording 91·37 miles per hour), he had twice failed as a car

The most powerful American car of its day – Henry Ford standing by his 999 in 1902.

manufacturer and persuaded businessmen to back him only with the greatest difficulty. Ten years later he commanded forty per cent of the domestic car market; ten years after that the company was valued at one thousand million dollars and Ford, with his son Edsel, owned every cent of it. By the time father and son died (in 1947 and 1943 respectively) they had amassed a combined personal fortune of $900 million. Only one task remained: to stop the government getting any. In this, too, they were successful.

And yet Henry Ford died an embittered, frustrated old man. Like another cantankerous and mulish Anglo-Irishman of his generation, George Bernard Shaw, Ford had made a slow start, sprung to fame, glory and riches in his fifties and sixties, and then clung to life, despite waning creative powers, with quirkish tenacity, praising vegetables and dictators. "The horse has virtually disappeared. The car is next and politics will follow," declared Ford on his 77th birthday. Hitler had given him a medal and Stalin later cabled: "One of the great industrialists . . may God preserve him." But the Ford Motor Company had become the ruined victim of the autocrat's delirium.

Nor did the Ford Foundation, established in 1936

to evade death duties, give him any pleasure. He ignored it. What it became after his death would have enraged him – liberal, cosmopolitan, a plunder box for the gasbags of social science. Himself a lifelong semi-illiterate who in his 50th year spelt 'coal' as 'cole' and 'much' as 'mutch', and who despised all education except the practical and vocational (hence the Henry Ford Trade Schools), Ford had announced that reading merely mussed up his mind. And yet when the Ford Foundation handed out an unprecedented $500 million in 1955 – *his* money, goddam it – half of it went to raising the salaries of the parasitical professariat.

"Consider the Lilies of the Field, how they grow they toil not neither do they spin . . ."

"Faith, Hope, Charity."

These words appear on the interior walls of the Dearborn farmhouse, now preserved in Greenfield Village, where Henry Ford was born in 1863, the eldest of the six surviving children of William and Mary Ford. The son of a modestly prosperous and hard-working Michigan farmer who had emigrated from Ireland in 1847 (the family was originally from Devon), the young Henry caught sight of a steam traction engine 65

The Detroit Automobile Co. factory in 1899, with Henry Ford seated in one of only 25 vehicles to be built there.

at the age of twelve and never looked back. Instinctively attuned to the line of reasoning of any machine, Henry disregarded his father's admonitions and departed for Detroit in 1879, working as an apprentice in various machine shops, supplementing his earnings by mending watches, and emerging as an expert steam engineer. But his progress was by no means meteoric: although in 1885 he was already working on an Otto four-cycle internal combustion engine, it was not until 1896 that he completed the two-cylinder, air-cooled car which he had been assembling in a brick shed behind his Bagley Avenue home. Three years later, having found backers to form the Detroit Automobile Company, he finally quit his job as chief engineer of the Edison Illuminating Company. The venture was not entirely successful; only twenty-five vehicles had been manufactured when the company went out of business in November 1900.

It was in 1908 that Ford finally produced the most famous and popular motor car in history, the car on which his fortune rested for the following nineteen years, the Model T, or Tin Lizzie. Standing 7ft. tall and

8ft. 4in. long, she cost $950 in 1909 but only $600 in 1913. According to popular legend, Ford virtually designed, made and assembled the Model T with his own hands. In reality, although his own vision of a cheap, reliable, mass-produced car was an indispensable factor in the birth of the Model T, he also displayed a flair for bringing together the best metallurgists, engineers, designers and production organisers available. (And for firing them on a whim.) Equally crucial was the dynamic presence in the company of a business genius called James Couzens, whose ability to advertise cars, fill order books and sell cars through an efficient, nation-wide network of dealers, inspired the Ford production team at Highland Park to astonishing feats of ingenuity and sustained effort. But in 1915 Ford and Couzens parted company, alienated by conflicting attitudes towards the war in Europe – Couzens, strongly pro-Ally, was outraged by Ford's public pacifism. Thus Ford lost the one man who had dared to give him hell. Nevertheless Couzens (who later became mayor of Detroit and a liberal U.S. senator) ultimately made a fortune out of the com-

Henry Ford (in jacket) with Thomas Edison and President Harding (both facing camera) during a camping trip in 1921.

pany, selling Henry Ford his $1 shares for $2500 each and thereby raking in a cool $29 million. Ford's passion for absolute control through total ownership of the company's stock ultimately cost him $105 million.

His great social achievement was to transform the lives of rural Americans. In the early years of the century farmers had so hated the city slickers who brought death and destruction with their cars to country roads that they built barricades, dug ditches, and even staged ambushes to keep the automobile at bay. But while Ford was progressively cutting the price of his cars the farm products index rose by fifty-two per cent in ten years – this factor more than any other set the seal on his success. Farmers adapted Model T's to carry livestock and hay, and to furnish power to grind grain and saw wood. The Model T shrank America, played the beloved fool's role in the comedies of Chaplin and the Keystone cops, was tinkered with, talked to, transformed into ploughs and campers, and carried Mr and Mrs Sinclair Lewis from Minnesota to California. The story is told of the old

timer from Colorado who insisted that when he passed on his Model T should be buried beside him: "the darned thing pulled me out of every hole I ever got into."

In 1927 the Model T was finally laid to rest by the pleas of Ford's associates, notably his son Edsel, by the alarming rise of Chevrolet and Chrysler, and by the feminine demand for a car with a little elegance and comfort, a car which could be started without the strength of an amazon and without risk of breaking your wrist if you heaved the crank down instead of up. Amid the kind of coast-to-coast excitement generated in our own time by the film *Jaws*, Ford unfurled the Model A: bigger, faster, prettier. No longer did Henry Ford insist, "They can have any colour they want, so long as it's black". Within a fortnight 400,000 firm orders were in the books and Douglas Fairbanks wired from Hollywood: "Mary [Pickford] uses new Ford in preference to all her other cars." Franklin D. Roosevelt bought one. Ford had done it again.

But in reality there was no way of repeating the success of the Model T. In 1910 there had been one car 67

The millionaire's apprenticeship: Henry Ford (left) and co-workers at the Edison Illuminating Company works, 1893.

for every forty-four American households; by 1930 there was one for every 1·3 households. Alfred Sloan of General Motors and Walter Chrysler of Chrysler were proving themselves to be geniuses of mass production every bit the equal of Ford in a fiercely competitive market where diversification and styling held the key to success. During the next twenty years the Ford Motor Company steadily lost ground.

Even so, it was a formidable empire that Ford had created, with the help of his handsome, work-hungry and ruthlessly efficient grand vizier of production, Charles Sorensen, a Danish-born tool-and-die maker who had joined the company in 1904, at three dollars a day, and had subsequently ascended like a fire-darting Apollo to a position of legendary power – the awful scourge of supervisors, terror of the assembly lines, Mr Ford's undisputed Right Hand Man. The empire now embraced sixteen coal mines in Kentucky and West Virginia, a large railroad system, millions of acres of land rich in timber and iron ore, a fleet of Great Lake boats, and a 2·5 million acre rubber plantation in Brazil, known as Fordlandia, into which $20 million was ultimately poured. Ford was able to intimidate his suppliers into more docile postures by threatening to become self-sufficient in steel, glass and rubber tyre production.

And then there was the foreign empire: Ford of Canada, Ford of Britain – in 1911 a Model T stunted its way to the top of Ben Nevis and the Ford Popular, at a price of £100, became in 1935 the most popular of British cars. The anti-Bolshevik Ford also did $40 million worth of business with Soviet Russia where the term 'to Fordise' meant 'to Americanise'. When Sorensen visited the Putilov works familiar voices called out to him from every side, "Hello, Charlie" – the Reds had apparently spirited away a dozen Ford foremen on a dark Dearborn night.

"Wherever he goes the crowds press upon him as if he were a king . . . and thrust their petitions . . . into his ears." By 1914 Ford was the best known and best liked private citizen in America – his slow start had perhaps saved him from the muck-rakers and populist moralists who had savaged Rockefeller and J. P. Morgan, allowing him to pose as an anti-capitalist folk hero, the scourge of Wall Street. "There are economic laws, but who knows what they are? The bankers don't . . ." The demagogue who poses such questions need never answer them – and Ford never did, this "slight, boyish figure with thin, long sure hands, incessantly moving," as the revolutionary writer John Reed described him. Nevertheless, Ford's utterances, shaped into print by his amanuenses Samuel Crowther and W. J. Cameron, do yield a

Ford's first assembly line in 1913 – building magnetos at the Highland Park factory.

primitive theory of labour and value which shares with Marx's the assumption that only labour generates value, and with John Locke's the assumption that the productive entrepreneur is the supreme worker. Ford yearned to become an -ism; but only the Germans fully obliged with their reverence for 'Fordismus'.

The rugged virtues were selfevidently his: independence, stubborness, scorn of the big city. He spoke the language of the cracker-barrel philosopher, of the Bible belt evangelist, denouncing drink, tobacco and usury, yet explaining away inequality as a factor in nature with the remark: "The very poor are recruited almost solely from the people who refuse to think." Samuel Marquis, an acute observer who was Ford's erstwhile clergyman and employee, remarked: "I think he would rather be the maker of public opinion than the manufacturer of a million automobiles a year." He was, in fact, an exceedingly shrewd publicist: during the 1920s, some 1500 people wrote to him every day, mainly on personal matters.

Nor could the mighty afford to ignore him – both in peace and war, the Ford factories might save them. He met or corresponded with seven successive presidents, and there is no doubt that he would have liked to become the eighth. It was Woodrow Wilson who prompted him to run for the Senate in 1918. At the end of an excessively dirty campaign, during which Edsel Ford's apparent evasion of military service was thrown in his father's teeth, Ford was pipped at the post by his Republican rival, Truman Newberry. The following year Ford suffered an appallingly extended public humiliation when he brought a libel action against the *Chicago Tribune*, which had described him not only as an anarchist, but as an ignorant one to boot. During a protracted cross-examination covering all aspects of American life, literature and history, his ignorance was indeed exposed: he thought the American revolution had occurred in 1812 and that

The assembly line in action – one day's output from Highland Park, photographed in 1913.

Benedict Arnold was "a writer, I think". (But could his tormentors have designed a carburettor to save their lives?)

These experiences, following on his much-ridiculed voyage in the 'peace ship' *Oscar II* in 1915, permanently embittered Ford. His pride was wounded to the quick. Having sailed to Sweden in the company of such peacemongers as Madame Rosika Schwimmer, Jane Addams, and Oswald Garrison Villard, Ford had caught a cold in the head and rapidly made tracks for home, for terrain he understood. Jeering critics pointed out that two years later he had turned over his factories to the production of Liberty motors and Model T tanks, promising to refund his war profits to the government, but quietly omitting to do so. Despite the characteristically modest half-smile of the photographs, the slight deflection of the eyes out of an apparent shyness, his pride was now up. When ex-President Theodore Roosevelt arrived at the Detroit Athletic Club in 1916 and expressed through mutual friends the desire to meet Ford, the industrialist declined to make the ten-mile journey. Roosevelt, he insisted, was very welcome to visit him in Dearborn. Roosevelt also declined. Seventeen years later another, bitterly detested, Roosevelt invited Ford to call in at the White House and talk things over. Ford stayed home.

Ford's populism was of the most dangerous sort: narrow, bigoted, racist, at root profoundly authoritarian. "We have been unfaithful to the White Man's traditions and privileges," he declared in the *Dearborn Independent*, the weekly paper he purchased in 1918. "We have permitted a corrupt orientalism to overspread us . . ." On to Ellis Island were pressing the anarchistic scum of foreign lands, hordes programmed to destroy the United States. In May 1920 he launched in the *Independent* a ninety-one-week campaign dedicated to exposing the 'International Jew', the Protocols

71

of the Elders of Zion (already exposed as a forgery) and the fact that Jews were responsible for Bolshevism, Wall Street, alcohol profiteering, gambling, short skirts and rolled stockings, jazz and cheap Hollywood movies: "Father of Psychoanalysis a Jew". But when Aaron Sapiro, a Chicago lawyer whom the paper had accused of attempting to defraud American farmers on behalf of a Jewish international syndicate, sued Ford for defamation, Ford settled out of court. In July 1927 he announced his high regard for Jews, his deep regret that they had been cruelly slandered in his paper, and his own absolute innocence in the matter – his subordinates, evidently had been solely responsible.

Henry Ford and his young son Edsel, taken in about 1898.

This was typical of Ford. He never fired a man face to face. Invariably a hatchetman was assigned the dirty work. Hatchet quite literally – more than one senior executive learned that his services were no longer required when he found the ceiling of his office hacked away and his desk open to the sky.

Forty years after Ford's anti-Semitic campaign, his great-grand-daughter Anne married Giancarlo Uzielli, a Wall Street banker and a Jew. The present generation of Fords have short memories not by default, but by intention. Sadly enough, Ford's own anti-Semitic feelings were shared by the one genius to whom he

accorded lifelong admiration and devotion, his erstwhile employer and frequent camping companion, Thomas Edison. Ford transported Edison's Menlo Park laboratory, the cradle of the light bulb and the phonograph, from New Jersey to Greenfield Village, and then named the whole $30 million museum the Edison Institute.

Edison's prejudices were gospel to Ford. "The injurious agent in cigarettes," he wrote to 'Friend Ford' in 1914, "comes principally from the burning paper wrapper." Ford took the point. "If you study the history of almost any criminal," he explained to an ignorant world, "you will find he is an inveterate smoker." This was the man who told heart patients in the Henry Ford Hosptial to lie on the floor and eat celery, and in whose home a guest might be obliged to consume a six-course dinner, from hors d'oeuvre to coffee, entirely derived from Ford's soybeans, while the host (always an elegant dresser) sported a complete outfit of clothing made from the same source – minus the shoes.

From 1914 to 1920 Ford was a benevolent despot; thereafter, a despot. Not only did he hire more cripples, tuberculars, ex-convicts – and blacks – than other employers, he also enrolled 14,000 of his workers in open-air English classes in an attempt to improve the lot of the foreign-born. (Thirty-eight were dismissed for refusing to attend.) A new Sociological and Legal Department was created with a view to bringing the social, family and economic lives of the workers within a single paternalistic embrace.

But what gave the Ford Motor Company its universal reputation as the ideal employer was Ford's sensational announcement in January 1914 that he intended to share $10 million of profits with his workers and double their salaries to $5 (£1) a day. Most newspaper comments were enthusiastic: "Magnificent," declared the *New York World*; "Henry Ford's great gift was made to spread happiness," swooned the *San Francisco Examiner*. But the *Iron Trade Review* complained that his gesture was inconsiderate to other employers, while the *Wall Street Journal* accused him of applying biblical principles where they did not properly apply. Nonsense, said Ford: my workers will now be able to buy my cars.

A week after the announcement captured the world's headlines (his reduction of the working week to forty-eight hours was virtually ignored), 12,000 men, desperate for jobs, assembled outside the factory gate on a freezing January morning. The police drenched them with fire hoses.

The assembly line, of course, was the lynch-pin of 'Fordismus', of low cost mass production. "The idea,"

Ford the young visionary, by Norman Rockwell – one of a series for the 50th anniversary of Ford Motor Co. 1953.

wrote Ford, "came in a general way from the overhead trolley that the Chicago packers use in dressing beef" – but Sorensen said it came from Sorensen. The system was first fully operated in April 1913; within six months the time required to assemble one car was reduced from 9 minutes 45 seconds to 5 minutes 56 seconds. Today, programmed by computerised ticker-tape which dictates every variable, every accessory in every pre-specified car, Ford Mustangs come off the Rouge assembly line one a minute.

"I have been told by parlour experts," said Ford, "that repetitive labour is soul- as well as body-

destroying, but that has not been the result of our investigations." But hear it from the anarchist, the artist, John Dos Passos: "... less waste, more spotters, strawbosses, stool-pigeons (fifteen minutes for lunch, three minutes to go to the toilet . . . reachunder, adjustwasher, screwdown bolt . . . until every ounce of life was sucked into production and at night the workmen went home grey shaking husks)." It was so: Ford workers were often observed to fall asleep as soon as they boarded the bus, not waking up until long past their destination. Today things are better; after $7\frac{1}{2}$ hours work they leave in sound physical shape and 73 take a bus only as far as the car park. Union committeemen armed with stopwatches fight speed-ups every inch along the line. Company, union and workers are agreed that a man steps inside the plant not to expand his personality or his creativity, but to earn dollars, and interest in the psychological effects of remorseless, 'reachunderadjust' repetition is reduced to token proportions.

After 1920 the Ford regime was hell. Sorensen, P. E. Martin and other managers stalked the plant imposing a harsh, inhuman regimentation. And then came the Depression. Henry Ford cut his wages to $4 a day, slashed his labour force, and generally indicated that the slump was God's way of separating the men from the boys. "I have no patience with professional charity . . . The moment human help is systematised, it becomes a cold and clammy thing." At a time when people were lying in the gutters of Detroit, poisoned by food scavenged from refuse bins, at a time when nearly a third of the 250,000 living on the dole were Ford workers and their families, the Ford family drew $8·5 million in cash dividends from the company – and sent $140,000 of it to the Community Chest. In 1932, when a column of hunger marchers converged on the Ford factory, the Dearborn police opened fire, killing four. The Dearborn police never failed Henry Ford, just as the Flint police department gratefully accepted an armoury of weapons from General Motors.

To the rise of the trade unions, particularly the United Automobile Workers, the Detroit automobile industry responded with brutal aggression. Ford was the most brutal. "It is utterly foolish," he had declared in 1924, "for Capital and Labour to think of themselves as groups. They are partners." To prove the point, he equipped himself with a corps of 3000 hired gangsters, busted detectives and football players organised into a 'Service Department' under the iron fist of an ex-prizefighter and sailor called Harry Bennett. It was Bennett who garnished the payroll with such characters as Chester La Mare, the Al Capone of Detroit, and Joe Adonis, of Murder, Inc. From 1927 to 1945 Bennett was Henry Ford's principal confidant, agent provocateur, and hatchetman.

Edmund Wilson came upon these characters during a visit to Dearborn. "Like Ford, they part their hair in the middle . . ." UAW militants were pursued through the streets, beaten up at bus stops, in bars, in their own homes. American Legionnaires, professional red-baiters, and fascistic Black Legionnaires were commissioned to infiltrate union meetings and to slug women standing in picket lines. Fritz Kuhn, leader of the German-American Bund and the top Nazi in the

U.S., went on the Ford pay-roll; so did Dudley Pelley, leader of the Silver Shirts. In 1937 Ford thugs dressed in the inevitable blue serge suits and black hats seized a group of leading UAW organisers, notably Walter Reuther, future president of the union, pulled their jackets over their heads, thumped them to the ground, hauled them to their feet, repeated the treatment. Incriminating film was torn from the cameras of reporters, but one photographer got away – it was enough.

Henry Ford detested the New Deal, social security, the National Labour Relations Board (which chronicled and condemned his illegal actions), and the automobile code of the National Recovery Act, which he refused to sign. Strangely enough, a *Fortune* opinion poll taken in 1940 found that 73 per cent. of Americans regarded him as 'helpful to labour', even more 'helpful' than John L. Lewis, leader of the Mine Workers and the CIO. "His face in repose," reported James Bone in the *Manchester Guardian* after an interview with *der Alte*, "has that remote look we call ascetic and is seen frequently in religious people." By 1941, when Ford finally surrendered and signed a contract with the UAW, some 4000 workers had been fired from his plants for suspected union activity. Indeed, the brutality had been almost worse in Dallas and Kansas City than in Ford's gigantic River Rouge plant, situated on the border between Dearborn and Detroit, and known universally as 'the Rouge'.

The life of a Ford worker today is very different. National recession is his main enemy: as of July 1975, over 25 per cent. of the company's workers are laid off. But once at work, an assembly line worker can expect to take home $14,000 a year, a foreman up to $18,000. Above all, the union has anchored a man's tenure to his seniority. So good is the Supplementary Unemployment Benefits programme in the event of short-term lay-offs (it collapses under the weight of a major recession like the present one) that redundant workers take home 95 per cent. of their normal pay minus $7·50, the consequence being that senior workers, by strict rule the last to be laid off, have grown restless during the long, hot summer months, sweltering in welder's masks, in the steel mills, in the tool and die shops, thinking of all those young bloods out fishing and shooting in the Michigan marshlands, or boating on the lakes, or cruising through Florida with some girl. Inevitably, since Americans are an eminently practical people, 'reverse seniority' has now been introduced, according the older hands priority in the queue to be laid-off.

"The man who dies rich dies disgraced," said Andrew Carnegie. Henry Ford was not impressed. Al-

The third generation: Benson (left), Henry II (centre) and William Clay Ford with their sister Josephine (seated right) and their mother Mrs Edsel Ford.

though he endowed a hospital in Detroit which bears his name, during the last thirty years of his life he gave away only $36 million to philanthropies. Rockefeller gave as much to the University of Chicago alone. No great universities, libraries or art galleries did Ford endow, and Greenfield Village has to be viewed mainly as a monument to himself.

We have seen how easy it was to make a fortune in America before the Second World War: labour was cheap and plentiful, the unions were weak, taxes were ridiculously low. Then came the spirit of the New Deal. In 1935 Congress passed an Act taxing inherited wealth at 50 per cent. over $4 million, at 70 per cent. over $50 million. Henry Ford at once recognised the stratagem for what it was: a conspiracy of Jewish Communists and Wall Street bankers, aided and abetted by GM and Chrysler, to destroy the White Knight of Dearborn. But Henry Ford was always a poor loser: he hired a thousand lawyers.

The lawyers finally realised that what the Ford family desired to do above all else was to endow a mighty foundation dedicated to 'human betterment'. This idealism ultimately saved the Fords from paying $321 million in death duties on the estates of Henry and Edsel. The company's stock was rescheduled, with 95 per cent. classed as 'A', and earmarked for the Ford Foundation (tax exempt). The remaining 5 per cent., 'B', would remain within the family. But only Class B stock would carry voting power. Furthermore, death duties on the family's Class B stock would be paid out of the Foundation's Class A stock.

By an ironic twist, one year after Henry's death, the anti-New Deal 80th Congress passed an amendment which rendered tax-exempt half of any estate where a spouse survived the deceased. I asked Henry Ford II, a large, genial, sun-tanned person with a noticeable air of prosperity about him, whether his family felt any resentment about the law of 1935. "What law?" he replied.

Behind Henry Ford II's desk are separate photographs of his father and grandfather. But in all the photographs which picture them together, the father always assumes the active, dominant posture while the son observes dutifully, his eyes limpid and passive, his hands clasped politely behind his back. Henry had given Edsel a million dollars in gold on his 21st birthday and made him president of the company five years later, but the son's almost angelic loyalty seems to have maddened the autocrat into re-doubling the humiliations, the constant countermanding of Edsel's orders. By every account Edsel was a fine man, generous, tolerant, morally courageous. One incident in particular illustrates this last quality.

Edsel Ford and his wife Eleanor were always generous patrons of the arts, and to this day both the Detroit Institute of Arts and the Symphony Orchestra owe much to the perseverant and self-effacing benefactions of Mrs Edsel. In 1932, acting on the advice of Dr Wilhelm Valentiner, director of the Institute and artistic consultant to the family, Edsel commissioned the Mexican Marxist artist Diego Rivera to paint a huge mural, extending over four walls of the Institute, on the theme of Detroit Industry. What emerged was not merely a striking work in the post-Cubist style seen also in Léger, with blocked-out toilers locked into a complex montage of machinery, but also an unambiguous condemnation of white imperialism and class exploitation, of the cold greed of the bourgeoisie, whom Rivera depicts crowded pig-like into a stall, in furs and crucifixes, watching the workers sweat dividends.

Inevitably a storm broke when the mural was first displayed. Catholics and conservatives alike demanded that it be obliterated, whitewashed. But Edsel and his fellow arts commissioners stood firm, insisting that "no other artist in the world could have painted murals of such magnitude and force."

Twenty years later Henry Ford II faced his own Diego Rivera trial in the shape of the Fund for the Republic. (When I mentioned the episode to him his expression clouded slightly, perhaps out of forgetfulness; a successful businessman knows over which of his shoulders the horizon is blurred.) At that time, in the early 1950s, the Ford Foundation's trustees seemed to be moving in contrary directions. On the one hand, money was being funded to the CIA-supported Congress for Cultural Freedom – Henry Ford II was personally pumping money into Radio Free Europe – but on the other hand the Fund had almost absent-mindedly given birth to a $15 million subsidiary called the Fund for the Republic.

Headed by the youthful and provocatively liberal former Chancellor of the University of Chicago, Robert M. Hutchins, the Fund had sponsored a wide range of studies and reports exposing the political purges then pulverising almost every profession. *The Tablet*, organ of the Brooklyn Catholic Archdiocese, screamed that "the living members of the Ford family" should be ashamed to stand by while "the inheritance of the great progenitor" was used "to sabotage efforts to expose the Communist conspiracy." Another group warned: "Do you own a Ford, Mercury, or Lincoln?" The American Legion and the House Committee on Un-American Activities joined in the chorus of denunciation. Ford dealers were burning up the lines to Dearborn while Ford

Edsel Ford, Henry's son and heir, skating at Dearborn, c. 1930.

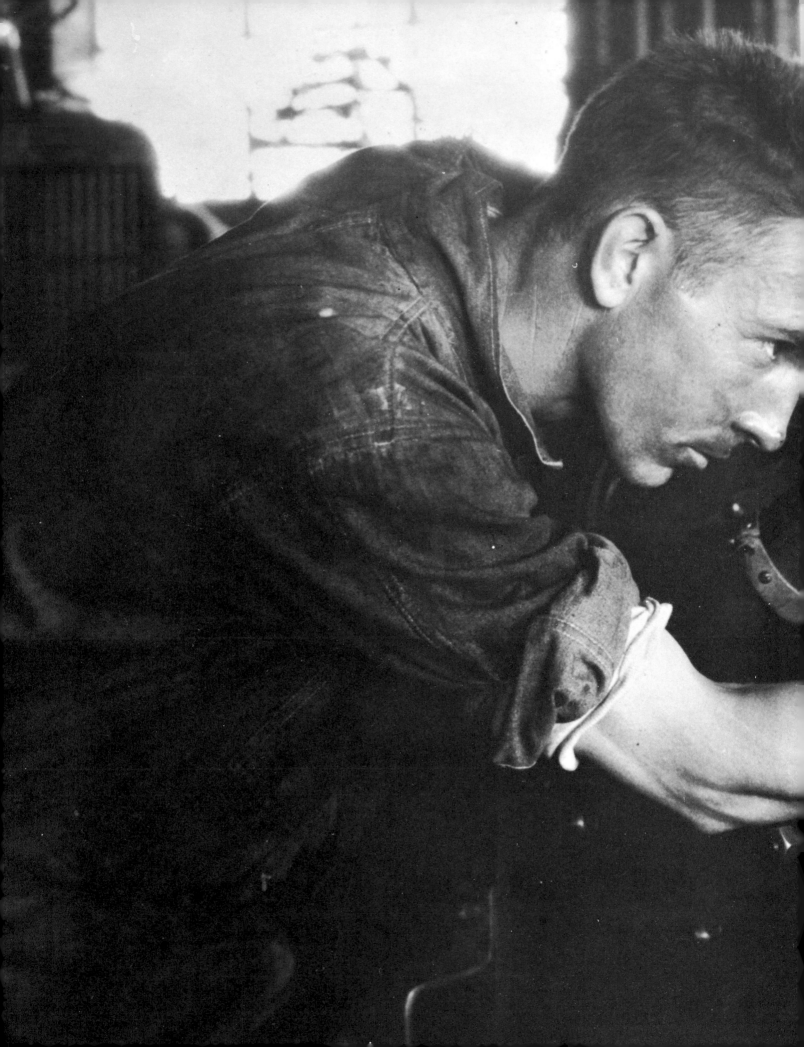

A craftsman of the twentieth century – the auto-engineer.

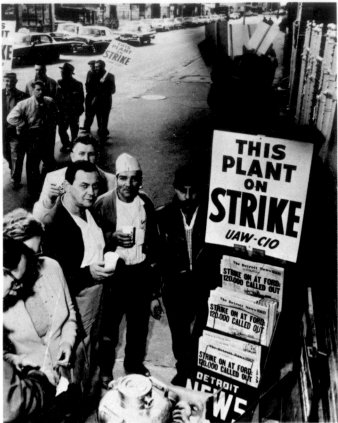

Brilliant though his industrial methods were, Ford's relations with the men who actually made the cars were appalling. In the Depression and the years after, mistrust between unions and management turned to open hostility.

STRIKE CALL!
To FORD ROUGE WORKERS:

Effective today, Wednesday, April 2nd, a strike is in effect at the Rouge plant of the Ford Motor Company.

The Demands of The Strikers Are:

Immediate reinstatement of all workers discharged for union activities.

A general wage increase. A seniority system.

Abolition of Ford spy system and service department.

Recognition of the UAW-CIO as the spokesmen of the Rouge workers and negotiation of a contract covering wages, hours, overtime, grievances, speed-up and other matters of importance to the Ford workers.

ALL WORKERS REPORT FOR PICKET DUTY. All picketing must be peaceful and disciplined.

By keeping our ranks UNITED, VICTORY WILL BE OURS!

United Automobile Workers of America, CIO.
R. J. THOMAS, President
GEORGE F. ADDES, Secretary-Treasurer
MICHAEL F. WIDMAN, Jr., Director,
Ford Division.

CIO IS BEHIND YOU
ONWARD TO VICTORY!

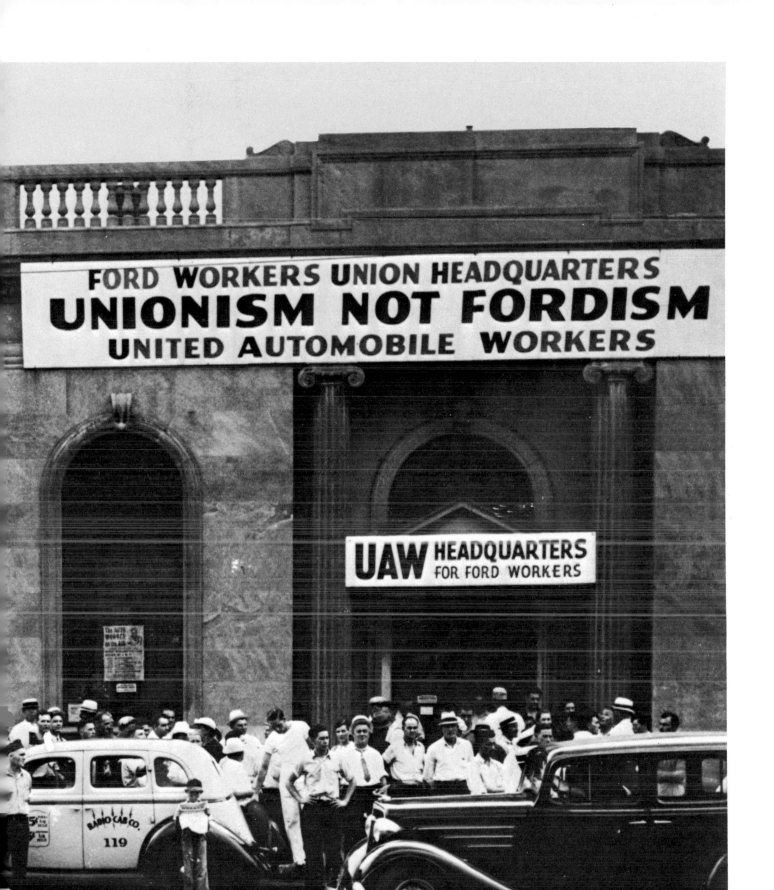

Battle of the Overpass: violence is close at hand at the Ford River Rouge plant, 1937, as Ford guards, on the left, adv

group of four officials of the United Automobile Workers.

executives were drubbing the Foundation's staff in New York as if they were day labourers hired by a spare-parts subsidiary.

Chairman of the Company, chairman of the Foundation, Henry Ford II faced his Diego Rivera. In December 1955 he publicly dissociated himself from the Fund: "Some of its actions, I feel, have been dubious in character and inevitably have led to charges of poor judgment." Today he says: "You have to remember that we run our business every day of the week through 6000 dealers, selling cars. The Rockefellers don't run a business in that sense."

By 1944 Ford's giant Willow Run plant, designed by Cast Iron Charlie Sorensen, was turning out one Flying Fortress an hour, Stalin was cabling his gratitude for Ford trucks, and the world had concluded, "Henry Ford has done it again". The reality, as Washington knew, was chaos and strife. Like his friend Colonel Lindbergh, in whose company Ford had twice been up in an aeroplane, and whom he had latterly taken on as a consultant, Ford was an America Firster who refused to manufacture Rolls-Royce aero engines for Britain in 1940 and bitterly denounced "that man" – Franklin D. Roosevelt – for inveigling America into the war. Imagine Ford's chagrin when William Knudsen, whom he had fired 20 years earlier for no good reason, and who had subsequently taken over General Motors, was appointed chief of war production. And picture a shrunken, scowling Ford squeezed into the rear seat of a car between FDR and his Mrs, the darling of the commies and the kikes, when the president regally inspected Willow Run amid the thunderous applause of the workers. Indeed, the old man was no longer *compos mentis*; in 1942 he told Sorensen: "Charlie, there's one man I don't want to see any more. You must get rid of Knudsen."

After Edsel Ford died of ulcers in 1943, half-driven to his grave by the autocrat, a period of furious intrigue followed. Transferring his suspicions from his son to his grandson, Henry I signed a secret codicil to his will, vesting control of the company for ten years after his death in a board of directors which Bennett would dominate. But in 1945 Mrs Edsel Ford, supported by her mother-in-law Clara Ford, a gentle, unassuming lady who loved Christianity and roses, threatened to sell her stock unless the old man abdicated in favour of her son. This was the sacred *voting* stock, the jealous preserve of the family. Henry Ford abdicated.

When Henry II became president of the company in 1945, at the age of twenty-eight, the company was losing nine million dollars a month, Bennett was boss, 83

Ford violence: the funeral of four hunger marchers shot in 1932.

Ford violence: the victim of a Ford organising battle in 1941.

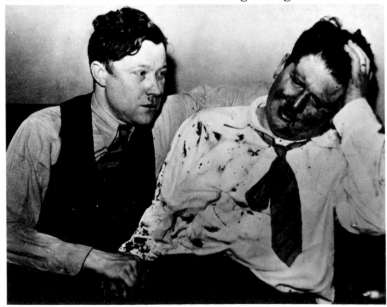

Battle of the Overpass: sequel to the picture on the previous page. In the struggle between Ford men and UAW organisers,

n's Richard Frankensteen is beaten up. Far left: he is tended after the fight by Walter Reuther, later union president.

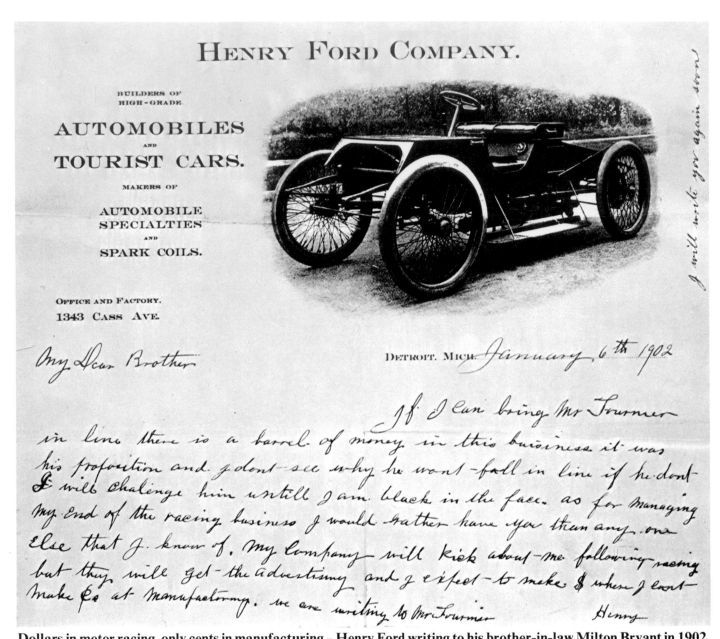

HENRY FORD COMPANY.

BUILDERS OF
HIGH-GRADE

AUTOMOBILES
AND
TOURIST CARS.

MAKERS OF

AUTOMOBILE
SPECIALTIES
AND
SPARK COILS.

OFFICE AND FACTORY.
1343 CASS AVE.

My Dear Brother

DETROIT. MICH. January, 6th 1902

If I can bring Mr Fournier in line there is a barrel of money in this business it was his proposition and I dont see why he wont fall in line if he dont I will chalenge him untill I am black in the face. as for Managing My end of the racing business I would rather have you than any one else that I know of. My company will kick about me following racing but they will get the advertising and I expect to make $ where I cant make ¢s at Manufactoring. we are writing to Mr Fournier

Henry

I will write you again soon

Dollars in motor racing, only cents in manufacturing – Henry Ford writing to his brother-in-law Milton Bryant in 1902.

and there seemed no way that the vessel could be hauled off the rocks by a bland, dough-faced young man who had playboyed his way from the Hotchkiss school to Yale, where he flunked courses in engineering and sociology – after presenting a fellow student's paper on Thomas Hardy as his own – and quit without a degree. As the enraged Harry Bennett spat out on the day that young Henry, carrying a gun and fearing for his life, dared to fire him: "You're taking over a billion-dollar organisation that you haven't contributed a thing to."

The story of Henry Ford II, in business terms, is one of achievement. He soon showed the ability to find and lure executives possessing the technical and administrative knowledge that he himself lacked: men like Ernest Breech of Bendix Aviation, modern-minded young dynamos like Robert McNamara, later president of Ford, Secretary of Defence, and now president of the World Bank. Ford negotiators, as Walter Borosh, assistant to the president of the UAW, recalled to me, were no longer bullish types liable 'accidentally' to swat your nose in pursuit of a fly during bargaining; or to shuffle grievances into two arbitrary piles, the one granted, the other denied.

Once post-war price controls had been eased, Ford overhauled Chrysler and zoomed into the crazy prosperity of the 1950s. In 1956 the company finally went public, releasing ten million shares, most of them owned by the Ford Foundation, and thus acquiring approximately one stockholder for every worldwide employee – close to half a million of each. But the family did not yield control. So adept was the reclassification of the shares, masterminded by Sidney Weinberg of Goldman, Sachs & Co., that the family maintained 40 per cent of the voting power owning only 12·1 per cent of the equity.

In what style do the Fords live? In 1915 grandpa and grandma built themselves a 56-room mock-Cotswold, modern-Tudor place called Fair Lane, buried in a 1240 acre estate of woodland. It's a hideous sight, with its turrets, crenellated roofs and fake chimneys. In a gorge below the house runs the same River Rouge which services the vast Ford plant to the east; Ford dammed the river to provide his castle with its own power plant, but on the night he died in 1947 the river had flooded and the Promethean of the autoelectric age expired by candlelight.

Turning his back on the golf course, stables, swimming pool and bowling alley that his parents added to Fair Lane to keep him at home, Edsel married Eleanor Clay and built himself another Cotswold mansion, on Grosse Point Shores, its garden fronting on to Lake St Clair. When their sons Henry II, Benson and William Clay (who owns the Detroit Lions), with their daughter Josephine, who all live close by, gathered one day in Mrs Eleanor Ford's drawing room to receive us, we found them friendly, direct, unpretentious.

Henry II's house I have not seen, but it is reported to contain a modern art collection almost equal to his mother's, with paintings by Van Gogh, Matisse, Degas, and Renoir's *Coco*. In the Fifties he was a big spender in the international auction rooms, paying £270,000 at Sotheby's for a Gauguin and a Cézanne at a single session. Even so, Mr Ford's knowledge of such matters is possibly less than profound; he did manage to describe a Cézanne oil painting in his mother's dining room as a water colour, and when asked who painted a large abstract hanging outside his private dining room in Ford headquarters, he distinctly replied, through his plastic-tipped baby cigar, "The name's on the bottom."

There was an occasion, in 1920, during a slump in the art market, when the famous dealer Lord Duveen drummed up a syndicate and put together a lavish, three-volume collection of reproductions with which to entice Henry Ford. Duveen was most courteously received at Fair Lane by Ford who, delighted by the gift, called out: "Mother, come in and see these lovely pictures." When the distraught Duveen tried to persuade Ford to buy the originals, Ford was baffled: why should he want to have two copies of the same picture?

Sartorially very elegant, but beginning to show his hamburgers, Henry II has an enviable record of fun-loving from the shooting glens of Scotland to the African safari belt to Rio via London and Sardinia, where permission to build a house has just been refused. His eldest daughter Charlotte was briefly married to the Greek tycoon Stavros Niarchos, by whom she had a daughter. The Aga Khan, Prince Rainier - not exactly old Henry Ford's style, though he did meet the British royal family. Most especially not in the style of the Catholic-hating old man was young Henry's conversion to Catholicism before he married his first wife, Anne McDonnell, in 1940. In In 1965 they were divorced and the Catholic Archdiocese of Detroit announced their excommunication. It is hard to conclude that these events leave much of a mark on Henry II.

In 1972 his salary was $264,567, plus a bonus of $610,000, plus annual dividends of over $3 million. Not so bad, and he's not complaining, particularly as the American weeklies, perhaps not unmindful of the value of automobile advertising, revere him as the most loose-tongued master industrialist in the nation, and call him 'super star' (*Fortune*, May 1973), etc. After the Detroit riot in 1967, in which forty-three people were killed and tanks were called in to defend General Motor's headquarters, *Look* panted: "To the riot-racked residents along Detroit's 12th Street, Ford is the white man who cares." (Maybe, but don't bother to ask a Ford chauffeur to drive you down 12th Street, or through the Livernois-Fenkell area. Henry Ford II says he touches the rim of the ghetto during his 35-minute drive to Dearborn every morning, "but of course I don't go right through the middle of it.")

After the Detroit riot, the worst civil commotion in American history, with columns of smoke visible from miles around, the white man who cares was among the city burghers who rallied to form a bridge-building receptivity centre of conflict resolution called New Detroit. For a while Henry II outpaced the chairmen of GM and Chrysler in talking to Black Panthers about why they so hated poverty, unemployment, lousy housing, lousy schooling, police racism and brutality. Today housing and schooling conditions in Detroit are no better than in 1967, unemployment is much higher (over 50 per cent in the ghetto), the middle class have fled to distant suburbs, businesses have quit, the tax base is shrinking, and the pawnbrokers (Al's Loan Office - 3 per cent per month) are thriving. Henry Ford II, still nominally a vice-president of Detroit Inc., has frankly lost interest in it. Black crime in Detroit, he reminded me, is largely black v. black: "A lot of it's drug-related."

Newspapers which knock Detroit - and he makes the point with some emphasis - don't help. Particularly not to be knocked at the present time is his current extramural enthusiasm, a project in which he himself has been the pacemaker, and which is already rising in steel-girdered splendour on the Detroit riverfront. Called the Renaissance Center, it is designed to act as an economic catalyst in a depressed area, and to make a profit. Whether a 70-floor hotel, four office-block towers, and a complex of high-income apartments and luxury shops (a Dunhill's, for example, he suggests) is precisely what the city's 700,000 blacks need is open to question. But then, as a Ford official pointed out, building lowcost housing simply is not commercially viable.

Before I went to interview Mr Ford I spent a couple of evenings in the hotel homeworking on a bundle of recent Ford interviews obligingly provided by the public relations department. But the pencil poised to mark the salient point, the root assertion of outlook, the truly distinctive attitude, remained poised. He says a lot but what does he say? He is against pollution; favours energy control; wants more national planning; believes in free trade. On the other hand, pollution control is ruinously expensive, conventional cars are here to stay, governmental controls are a nuisance, and something must be done about the Japanese. All his gear shifts seem to lead back into neutral.

He is different, of course, from his grandfather, but how different? Said Henry I: "Without the most rigid discipline we would have the utmost confusion." Says Henry II: "Participatory democracy is fine in theory, but hard to put into practice . . . Protest has its place, but right now our country seems to have all the protestors it can use. What we really need are more people who are willing to come inside the system . . ."

This successful industrialist – Ford now ranks third among American manufacturing companies – can dismiss any executive on a whim but is without a trace of arrogance. "You want to ask me philosophical questions? Those are the ones I'm no good at." Of course he cares. He has given generously to black organisations and in 1967 he did more than his share in finding work for 146,000 of the 'hard-core unemployed' across the country. But almost half had dropped out within a year. He sighs a bit: "They just couldn't get themselves up in the morning."

So it goes. One black who got up very early on a particular South African morning was the hero of Athol Fugard's play, *Sizwe Bansi is Dead*. Yes, sir. Up before dawn to scrub out that factory and get fitted for that spotless overall he'd never seen before, whole place humming with hygiene. For the Big Man was coming. Henry Ford II. He came. But then he went away and everything went back to normal.

Henry Ford at 80, on the steps of his winter house at Richmond Hills Plantation, Georgia.

GUGGENHEIM

Bruce Chatwin

Opposite: Meyer Guggenheim in 1889 – father of the family, chairman of the board.

Leadville, Colorado, boom town base of the Guggenheim fortunes in the 1880s.

The Jewish Cemetery at Salem Fields, Long Island, is approached through a grandiose portico of Ancient Egyptian inspiration. Urns, arches, obelisks, temples and kiosks mark the resting places of the dead. Aside from the Pharaonic, the styles are Doric, Ionic, Solomonic, and Hindoo; the Gothic, for its association with Anglo-Saxon Protestantism, is rare. Rare too is the image, banned by the articles of Judaism. Among the tombs there are some real monstrosities, but most have clean lines, bare lettering and a robust mineral permanence, and give the impression of bracing austerity. In the north-west corner two celebrated New York families glower at each other. The Seligmans, bankers and first German Jewish millionaires in America, occupy a domed pantheon with a window of the Smashing of the Altars of Baal. The Guggenheims, metal kings extraordinary, lie in a free version of the Tower of the Winds at Athens, their bodies stowed behind marble panels sculpted to resemble hanging drapery. In the mosaic roof are some entwined verses of the Psalms, including the line: "The Lord is my Shepherd. I shall not want."

Here lies Meyer Guggenheim, the founder of the fortune and son of Simon, a Swiss tailor, who came to America in 1848; his wife and step-sister, Barbara; and six of his eight sons, Daniel, Isaac, Murry, Simon, Solomon and William, all, except the last, equal partners in the gigantic mining enterprise known as Guggenheim Brothers. The two missing sons are Robert, knocked down as a boy by a horse cart in Philadelphia, and Benjamin, who drowned on *The Titanic*. Alongside the Brothers are various sisters and wives, including Florette, widow of Benjamin, who overlooked her husband's infidelities and chose to lie with her brothers-in-law rather than her Seligman brothers a hundred feet away.

The third generation is patchily represented since, by then, the Guggenheim family was coming apart. The latest addition is Harry Frank, son of Daniel, an aviator, ex-ambassador to Cuba, financier of the first rockets, racehorse owner and conservative newspaper proprietor. He will be one of the last Guggenheims buried there. Descendants of Meyer Guggenheim are alive and well, but *they* have names like Sinbad Vail, Wanda Weyshan, Earl Castle Stewart, Oscar Straus III, Peter Lawson-Johnston and Iris Love. The last is an irrepressible archaeologist who excavated the right index finger of the *Venus de Milo*.

The Guggenheims' Swiss origin tended, marginally, to set them apart from the clannish German Jewish families of New York, who intermarried and called themselves 'Our Crowd' – the Seligmans, Kuhns,

Main Street, Leadville. The Guggenheim's mine was valued at over $14 million.

Loebs, Schiffs, Lehmans, Warburgs, Lewisohns, Sachses and Goldmans – who usually stuck to the traditional occupations of Jewry, as private bankers, brokers, traders and entrepreneurs. The Guggenheims left 'Our Crowd' somewhat aghast. They had greater faith in the possibilities of America, and instead of confining themselves to abstractions of the money market, assembled a mining empire from Alaska to Chile and the Congo. They made more money faster than anyone in America with the exception of Henry Ford. But they were always out on a limb, and, at the apex of their fortune, seem to have put themselves into voluntary dissolution.

Their forebears lived at Lengnau, the 'ghetto' of Switzerland, in the Canton Aargau, near Zürich. The first recorded Guggenheims were the Jew Maram and his son Jakob, whom the Diet of Baden, in 1702, accused of owning his dead father's house and a vineyard he had taken in lieu of a debt. Officially the ghetto Jew was a "tolerated, homeless person, not to be expelled", condemned by Christian dogma and his own tradition to exile and blamed personally for killing Christ. A Jew could own neither house, nor field, nor animals, nor vegetable garden. He had to buy all food with cash. He could ply no manual trade, nor smelt gold or silver. He could buy no dressed stone or hewn timber, only rotten logs for fires. Three loopholes were permitted for his sustenance: peddling, tailoring and the cursed occupation, usury.

All his life Jakob Guggenheim lobbied for the end of the restrictions, dodged the attacks of Christians and, by 1840, was a *parnas*, or elder of the Synagogue, respected inside the Jewish community and out. Two of Jakob's four sons, Isaac and Joseph, already exhibited the tenacity and nervous instability of the American Guggenheims. Isaac, the grandfather of Meyer Guggenheim, lived to be 85; was the *kozin*, or treasurer of the congregation, and made a small fortune as a money-lender. His orthodoxy and self-importance earned him the nickname of 'Old Icicle'. Joseph was a brilliant and eccentric Talmudist, who was tempted to live in gentile Zürich by an unscrupulous pastor, with whom he had a marathon theological discussion that ended, 16 years and two nervous breakdowns later, with his conversion to Christianity, collapse and death. The Guggenheims blotted Joseph's name off the family roll as a warning against losing one's Jewishness.

After the Congress of Vienna, the Jews of Europe had watched their hopes for emancipation squashed in a round of reaction and ghetto-burning. In 1847, a year of revolutionary stirrings, Simon Guggenheim, 93

The gate to America: a Jewish girl from Russia arriving at Ellis Island.

A Jewish immigrant from Europe: the Guggenheims arrived from Switzerland in 1847.

the tailor of Lengnau and son of 'Old Icicle', asked permission to marry the widow Rachel Meyer. The authorities turned him down and forced the couple to live in sin. His son Meyer, a good-looking boy of twenty with chestnut hair and glittering eyes, was restless. In America there was free trading, bank credit, private property, universal education and travel without internal passports. Above all, one could shed there the self-inflicted restrictions of Old Judaism. So in the autumn the widow Rachel dug into her savings, and the Guggenheims and Meyers, all fifteen of them, decamped, and, after a dreadful winter crossing, came to Philadelphia, the City of Brotherly Love, a place without a ghetto.

The great German Jewish families of America distinguish whether their founder started as a pedlar or trader with a horse and cart. The Guggenheims were foot-pedlars, without even the money to start a tailor's shop. Father and son hawked boot-polish, laces, needles, stove-polish, ribbons and glue. Old Simon's beat was downtown Philadelphia. Meyer tramped the anthracite districts of Pennsylvania. On Fridays they reunited in their tiny house, a ritual they did not discard when they were multi-millionaires.

Meyer's fortune began with a stove-polish which he invented to supplant a brand that blackened the hands of complaining housewives. Simon brewed up the mixture in the backyard; Meyer was its travelling salesman. After four years in America he married his step-sister, Barbara, with whom he had fallen in love on the Atlantic crossing. She was nineteen, pale-skinned, auburn haired and grey-eyed, not beautiful, but with a serene expression that made everybody love her. Between 1854 and 1872 she mothered eleven children and, as the family grew, the couple compulsively moved house to grander and more convenient neighbourhoods; like most immigrants on the way up, they never anchored themselves to one place.

Nor did Meyer Guggenheim confine himself to any one craft or trade. He launched businesses and left them, with profits intact, whenever a better opportunity arose. He was honest and scrupulous, and at times a little ruthless in a ruthless age. He speculated on foodstuffs to feed the Northern Army on the Potomac. He opened a grocer's shop, but found the wholesale hardware business more profitable. In one devastating manoeuvre he broke the monopoly of a company that manufactured lye, and, after winning a court case, allowed himself to be bought out for $150,000. Once he made $300,000 on the depressed, and later booming, shares of a Kansas railroad.

He disciplined his sons with the birch and instilled
96 them with business principles they did not forget. He

The men who made the Guggenheims rich: workers at a mine in San Miguel County, Colorado.

The American miner (left) and the Jewish financier: a characteristic press attack on Guggenheim operations.

wanted for them the best possible place in America, and largely ignored the social questions that troubled them later and tormented the third generation. For him America was that magical system that, in affirming the equality of all men, allowed the clever ones to make money so fast. Yet the sufferings of his people had conditioned him to value Jewish cohesion and push. He mistrusted gentiles, never really confided in them, and examined every deal for its seamier side. He knew how to buy the right man, and when he had served his usefulness, how to be rid of him. Yet he was no Jewish fanatic. He took no great trouble to go to the synagogue or get involved in Jewish community affairs.

By the Seventies the condition of Jews in Switzerland had taken a turn for the better, and one of Barbara's uncles had invented, or bought, a machine that made lace frills for collars and cuffs. Meyer put up the money for a factory to supply the obvious American demand. He took on a partner, Morris Pulaski, to run the European business and teach his boys how Europeans managed their trade. Guggenheim and Pulaski called their laces 'Hamburg edgings', choosing Hamburg as their place of origin to put other American buyers off the scent. The four eldest sons – Isaac, Daniel, Murry and Solomon – crossed the Atlantic, finished their education and acquired a certain reverence for German culture and efficiency. By 1880 their grey-haired father could look forward to presiding over a prosperous, middle-class import-export business.

* * * * *

In the summer of 1877 an apparently trivial incident

at Saratoga Springs, New York, had changed the status of the Jew in America. The banker Joseph Seligman travelled there in his private railway carriage for his annual family vacation at the Grand Union Hotel, but the receptionist had instructions to turn him away. He had been there the year before and rubbed shoulders with East Coast society. He had raised bonds for Lincoln in Europe, had been offered the post of Secretary of the Treasury, and had made Mrs Potter Palmer giggle at White House dinners. And he had convinced himself that centuries of prejudice had broken down. The rich Jews of America were repeating the glittering success of the French Rothschilds as leaders of society.

He was either naïve or thick-skinned. For some time East Coast society, uncertain of its own pretensions, had been gearing itself to cope with its Jewish problem. Gentile circles were already murmuring about beaky noses. *Harper's Weekly* ran a cartoon showing "Catch 'Im and Pluck 'Im Bankers" and blamed anything that went wrong with the money market on the avarice of an unpatriotic cabal. Joseph Seligman returned to New York and did battle in the courts and Press, but his campaign misfired and only served to air a smouldering issue. From now on, American Jews found areas of privilege denied them. Hotels posted notices: "We have no Jewish patronage." Gentlemen's clubs black-balled Jews on principle. Business organised itself, in the name of Christianity, into tight anti-Jewish cliques.

* * * * *

Early in 1880 a Mr Charles Graham, a Pennsylvania Quaker, a grocer and amateur of mining booms, asked Meyer Guggenheim for a loan to finance a silver and lead mine at California Gulch, Leadville, Colorado. This valley had seen a gold rush, but the prospectors had panned it out. Then a visiting chemist found that the carbonate ores under the surface could be smelted to give silver and lead. Graham and some partners had bought two mines, the A.Y. and Minnie, from a prospector called A. Y. Corman, who was old and tired, unable to afford timber to shore up the mineshaft, and pestered by his wife, Minnie, to sell out. Guggenheim was not a professional money-lender and asked Graham for a partnership. His share cost him $5000, but by July he was not pleased with his investment. The A.Y. was yielding good ore, but at 70 feet the mineshaft struck water and had to be pumped dry. Meyer took the train to Leadville to inspect his property.

'The Cloud City', at 10,000 feet, was a rough town. Oscar Wilde had been there three years earlier, read the *Autobiography of Benvenuto Cellini* to the miners and saw the following notice: PLEASE DO NOT SHOOT THE PIANIST. HE IS DOING HIS BEST. Leadville had 120 saloons, 150 gambling dens and 35 whorehouses, in gingerbread style, down a street called Tiger Alley. It had the Tabor Grand Hotel, the Tabor Opera, a *Deutsche Zeitung* and six Jewish pawnshops. Graham calculated that the pumping operation, the timber and an increased payroll would cost another $25,000. Meyer grudgingly paid and bought out Graham's partners. Before leaving, he noticed his Hamburg edgings on sale and said: "That's about all I'll get out of Leadville."

A few weeks later his Philadelphia office got a cable: RICH STRIKE FIFTEEN OUNCES SILVER SIXTY FIVE PER CENT LEAD. But his prospect of an immediate million were dashed by news of the other kind of strike. The Leadville boom had magnetised miners and flooded the labour market. Disregarding the high cost of living in the mountains, the mineowners took advantage and cut wages from $5 a day to $2·75. The miners organised pickets, but the owners had some light cavalry sent in and the men had little chance of holding out.

In the autumn of 1881 Meyer got his first cheque for one month's production for $17,231. Within six months the A.Y. was giving 2000lb. of silver a day, and as late as 1890 the mine was valued at $14,556,000. The residents of Leadville resented "that damned smart Jew" but the town's *Herald Democrat* had the grace to compliment him on the greatest bonanza in the mountains. Meyer refused to sell for half a million. Interviewed in Denver he said: "I have seven sons and each will have a million dollars."

The sons – to say nothing of the daughters – were shaping up well. Meyer never tired of quoting them Aesop's fable: "Sticks bound together in a faggot hold. Individual sticks snap." All his boys would have equal shares in any partnership he planned for them. All votes would have to be unanimous. Isaac, the eldest, unimaginative but tenacious, had married a New York merchant's daughter and was in lace. Daniel was small and rather aggressive, a financial wizard and sufferer from stomach troubles. Murry was the most elusive. Solomon was utterly fearless. The younger sons, born after the family's first struggles, were a bit pampered and less reconciled to their Jewishness. Benjamin grew up a charming Edwardian swell. Simon was sad-eyed and reticent and more like his elder brothers. And William, the smallest of a small family, was a courageous dreamer, but possessed of a Napoleon complex.

Meyer squeezed the last cent from his mine. He beat the railroads down on freight charges. He evicted miners who squatted on his claims. If anyone sued him (as they often did) he removed the case to a

Peggy Guggenheim, art collector, in the garden of her Venetian palazzo.

A family of substance: Meyer Guggenheim surrounded by his family in 1889. The men (left to right): William (standi
The women: Cora (front row), Carrie (Mrs Isaac), Leonie (Mrs Murry), Barbara (Mrs Meyer), Jeanette, Florence (

on, Isaac, Meyer, Solomon, Murry, Daniel, Benjamin.
niel), Rose.

104   **Top: Florence, Mrs Daniel Guggenheim. Left: the family mausoleum at Salem Fields. Above: the Guggenheim Part**

om, Lower Broadway. The five desks, for the brothers who remained after William and Benjamin had left, are still there. 105

Federal court where the plaintiff stood little chance of winning. He resented the smelters' charges for processing ore, and saw – as John D. Rockefeller saw – that there was one way to make real money in mining: you had to own the mine and the processing plant and control the marketing of metal. Meyer decided to build his own smelter. He also moved to New York.

Benjamin was the first Guggenheim brother to get involved in his father's venture – the older brothers were in Europe or lace or both. He studied at the Columbia School of Mines and in the summer of 1883 worked at California Gulch, where he became an instant expert. He gave up his studies, preferring the real thing to theory and Tiger Alley to Columbia. In Leadville he befriended a Mr Edward Holden, 'The Prince of Silver Smelters', who ran a smelter that bore his name but over which he had no real control. Meyer sent Ben to work with Holden, and, in the upshot, the two agreed to float the Philadelphia Smelting and Refining Co. and build the biggest smelter in the world at Pueblo, Colorado. Work was unfinished when Holden withdrew complaining there was always a 'Guggy' in the way with unhelpful suggestions. The new hearthless furnace refused to work. Silver slumped from $1·35 to 95 cents a pound, and 'Guggenheim's Folly' became the stock joke of Western smeltermen. But again Meyer hired the right man, August Raht, a product of German mining schools, who rescued the wobbly concern and got the furnace working. Murry replaced Holden as manager. Will worked as a scaleman with wages of $100 a week. The Sherman Silver Purchase for the U.S. Treasury was announced, and the metal shot up in price. And the Guggenheims were so clever in handling their labour that the Pueblo smelter continued at full blast when strikes closed down all their competitors. Soon it was the most successful operation of its kind.

The older brothers shed the lace business and began ordering the younger ones about. Daniel, especially, became an overnight captain of the mining industry, and revealed a monumental ambition: to outsmart, outflank and consume their bigger competitors. The Guggenheims embarked on a now familiar strategy: you use the cheap labour and raw materials of undeveloped countries to depress the home industry, to force its wages and prices down, until you can afford to buy it up and sew it into your monopoly. First Dan encouraged the owners of the rich silver and lead mines in Mexico to send their ore to the Pueblo Smelter, and gave them most favourable terms. Threatened by the cheap ore, the Western mine-owners and smeltermen lobbied Washington and obtained the McKinley Tariff, which slapped a prohibitive tax on all imported ore. But this played into Guggenheim hands, and even the influential *Engineering and Mining Journal* predicted the next step: the building of American-owned smelters in Northern Mexico to compete on the world market. The oligarchy who controlled Mexico gave the *yanqui capitalistas* a gratifying welcome, and in 1890 the dictator Porfirio Diaz granted Dan a contract for *la exploracion y explotacion de minas de todo especie y la construcion de tres haciendas metallurgicas.*

The Guggenheims built two smelters, at Aguascalientes and Monterrey. Sol, and later William, aged 22, were in charge. They brought machinery from Chicago, built railroads, electric cables and dug canals. The difficulties were colossal: the Mexican peasant liked tequila and loathed work; the local mine owners became jealous; Will found his chief engineer dead from thirty knife thrusts and his staff in rebellion. But they got over the teething problems and Mexico did have one cardinal advantage: there were no strikes. Picked hussars herded the workers into the smelters at gun-point and sent agitators to an early grave. Soon the Mexican metal hit the world market.

* * * * *

In 1887, Mr Ward McAllister published the *New York Social Register*. Gentile New York had, at last, defined what it meant by society: basically the 400 people – none of them Jews – who squeezed into Mrs Waldorf Astor's ballroom. Mr 'Make-a-Lister' suggested that Jews might want to make a list of their own, but they did not rise to this bait. 'Our Crowd', however, did have its own idea of society, hermetically sealed, rich, worthy and rather dull. The Jewish plutocracy, with the Guggenheims among them, clustered together in stuffy mansions on the Upper West Side, and disdained the antics of Mrs Astor's 'butterflies'. In summer they went to Elberon, the Jewish Newport, a resort on a forlorn stretch of the New Jersey coast where distinguished Jewish bankers built overgrown cottages in a simple rustic style. When the Guggenheims arrived they changed the tone. Daniel built a Renaissance palazzo called *Firenze* after his wife Florence Schloss. Murry copied the Petit Trianon in white marble. Solomon bought a Moorish fantasy, which, it was said, suited his piratical, oriental temperament.

* * * * *

At the turn of the century American industry was consolidating into huge monopolies and Meyer Guggenheim said: "One day there will be one

Solomon Guggenheim, a businessman in middle age; his European forays as a patron of the arts came later.

smelting industry and it will be the Guggenheims'." But this was far from certain. In 1898 some eastern capitalists formed a gigantic Smelters' Trust to kill competition and control the wobbly price of metal. H. H. Rogers masterminded the operation; William Rockefeller backed it with the money of Standard Oil. The Trust invited the Guggenheims to join, but Meyer said: "They would control my smelter," and refused. Daniel did offer co-operation, but his price was control of the new company, and this was also refused. The Guggenheims had one smelter in the USA, two in Mexico and a rented one in Chile. His demand appeared ridiculous. However, the first priority of the new American Smelting and Refining Company was to run the Guggenheims into the ground, for going it alone and for being Jewish.

Dan cast round for allies. He chose William C. Whitney, a Protestant, a former Secretary of the Treasury, and a multi-millionaire, who was looking for business opportunities for his son. The two floated the Guggenheim Exploration Co., and yet Dan need not have worried. The Smelters' Trust was an inert colossus. Its directors bickered, milked the company, went back on their promise not to squash small operators, tried to destroy the Western Federation of Miners ("a lot of damned anarchists") and got bogged down in strikes. Meanwhile, the Guggenheims deferred to a Colorado court ruling for an eight-hour instead of a twelve-hour shift, and functioned without interruption. The popular Press hailed the Brothers as "Seven Giant-Slayers in One". A cartoon drew Rockefeller's bald pate as the head of an octopus. The Guggenheims then flooded the market with Mexican silver and lead. Within one year the Trust, a group of 27 smelters, had swallowed all its working capital, ran debts of seven million dollars and sued for peace. The Guggenheims and Whitneys took some shares, then rounded up more and more proxies, until Rogers woke to the fact that the enemy had control of his company. In fury he arranged a 'bear' market to depress the shares, but failed. The Guggenheims controlled the Trust, and had passed overnight from playing the role of saints to extortionists.

Barbara Guggenheim died of diabetes in 1900. She had kept her fractious family intact, and with her death the unit cracked. Ben and Will, who had spent their youth in the mines and rowdy-houses of the West, saw themselves as mine-owners and operators. They did not like the Whitney alliance or the family getting enmeshed in the intricacies of corporate finance. But they were outvoted and they drifted out of the partnership. Ben had married Florette Selig-

man, and had three daughters – Marguerite (the present Peggy Guggenheim), Benita, and Barbara Hazel. He took to high-life and mistresses in Paris. He sank his money in the International Pump Co. (which made the lifts for the Eiffel Tower) and left its affairs in chaos on his death. In her memoirs Peggy recalls his French marquise: "She was dark and resembled a monkey and had bad teeth which my mother always used to refer to as black." Florette wanted a divorce, but the two scandal-conscious families prevented her. Her marriage teetered on till Ben drowned on *The Titanic* in 1913, dressed up for the occasion in white tie and tails. Peggy remembers her shock seeing another of her father's girlfriends walking up the gangplank of the rescue ship – alone.

Will was difficult, a bit pathetic, but brave and attractive. His autobiography, written under the pseudonym of Gattenby Williams, and put out by his own Lone Voice Publishing Co., is a literary curiosity:

"At the turn of the century, Will had just passed his thirty-first birthday. He was a nice appearing young man. Well-proportioned, though only five feet four inches tall, he carried himself erect and with dignity. His hands were expressive, the gestures indicating refinement and a fundamentally artistic temperament . . . His hair, with a slight wave in it, was of a chestnut brown shade, tinged with grey . . . His eyes were greyish blue; his lips met in an even line, yet they seemed extraordinarily sensitive, belying the arduous responsibilities which had so long been his . . . Seeing Will's light complexion and his cast of features, one would not have surmised his Semitic ancestry."

The Brothers' unnecessarily spiteful treatment of Will was calculated to encourage the scandal they dreaded. Still pining for his mother, he had married Grace Brown Herbert, a Californian, a divorcee, a Gentile and a *demi-mondaine*. Dan told her that Will was a weakling and bought her off in return for a Chicago divorce. He packed Will off to Europe where he did the round of the casinos and fell out of love with Mrs Herbert. She returned eight years later, with her money exhausted, and blackmailed the family. Her lawyer claimed the Chicago divorce invalid, and that the children of Will's second marriage were bastards. The court subpoenaed all the brothers and the case bathed them in scandal until 1913.

Meyer Guggenheim was not pleased with his squabbling family and preferred the company of his son-in-law Albert Loeb. The sons had surpassed his wildest ambitions for them, but their extravagance alarmed him. As a widower he lived modestly. His

Falaise, the Guggenheim mansion at Sands Point, on Long Island Sound, built by Meyer's grandson Harry.

109

William Guggenheim and his wife Grace Herbert: the other Brothers paid off Grace in return for a quick divorce.

one luxury was a stable of trotting horses. He liked Wagner, and Gilbert and Sullivan. He did not much care for Temple Emmanu-El, but sent generous relief to survivors of the Kishinev pogrom in 1903. When Barbara died, his housekeeper, Hannah MacNamara, sued for $100,000 for breach of promise, saying he had been in "constant intimate association with her for 20 years". The veteran of the law courts fought the case and won. He died at Palm Springs in 1905; he had not recovered from an operation for which he refused an anaesthetic, saying: "You can't sell a Jew anaesthetics or life insurance." Instead he asked for a cigar and a gramophone to muffle the sound of the surgeon's knife.

Guggenheim Brothers (M. Guggenheim's sons, less Ben and Will) launched into their great scheme of expansionism. Their aim was to buy out or control every important mining enterprise in the New World in the rare metals of gold, silver, copper and lead. In 1903 they paid the world's largest salary to a single man. John Hays Hammond was a gentleman adventurer, and an old hand of South African gold

camps. The Guggenheims paid him $250,000 a year plus a quarter interest on any mine he introduced. For five years they and their shareholders reaped the benefits of his advice. They also took on his assistant Alfred Chester Beatty, and demanded of both "the most meticulous loyalty, the most scrupulous fidelity and sense of honour". On the Guggenheim payroll Hammond earned in two and a half hours what a pick miner earned in a year. His yachts, cars, houses and railway carriage, called *Kya Yami*, the Zulu for 'one of my homes', earned him the envy and irritation of the mining world.

From their walnut-panelled office at 120 Lower Broadway, with its five partners' desks, the Brothers expanded their empire, working inside and outside the Smelters' Trust. By 1907 they controlled 80 per cent. of the world's silver and dictated its price. They had the best gold mine in Mexico, La Esperanza; the last independent smelters, on Puget Sound; and on Beatty's recommendation they mounted a gigantic operation in the Canadian Yukon to dredge the gold-bearing sands of Bonanza Creek. Their most exotic

110

"How absurd! He wants his own country" – foreign capital, Guggenheims well to the fore, exploiting Mexico.

venture was their partnership with the ostentatiously Christian Thomas Fortune Ryan, to help King Leopold rescue his personal slave camp, the Belgian Congo, from Socialists in his own government.

Adolf Lewisohn, a rival Jewish financier of the mining industry, decided, earlier than the Guggenheims, that the spread of electric cables would make copper the coming metal. He had already taken a big stake in the Anaconda Mining Company's operation at Butte, Montana, when the Guggenheims also decided to go into copper. With an old-timer called Colonel Enos Wall and an unscrupulous Mormon, Dan Jackling, they developed, at Bingham Canyon, Utah, the largest open-pit copper mine in the world. There were several copper mountains in Nevada and Utah, but the ore was of very low grade. The Guggenheims solved the problem of dealing with it by constructing a smelter on the site. Its successor still belches pollution over the Salt Lake Valley.

Then they bought the purest lode of copper ever discovered. Some prospectors had spotted it as a patch of verdant green on an otherwise naked mountain at Kennecott, in the Wrangel Mountains, Alaska. When assayed it proved 70 per cent. pure, but the development costs were such that the Brothers had to combine with J. P. Morgan and the German Jewish banker, Jakob Schiff, to form the Alaska Syndicate. The Syndicate built railroads, bought steamships, fisheries, coalmines and forests, then ran into a snag. The Territory was the last hope of an American dream, a place where the frontiersman could be free. Gifford Pinchot, Theodore Roosevelt's chief forester, campaigned against the industrial spoilers. A cartoon showed a polar bear figure, with gloved hands and a Jewish nose, called the Morganheim; there was another creature called the Guggenmorgan. The conservationists accused the Syndicate of muzzling the Press and distorting facts, but they lost their case – the natural difficulties of Alaska were such that only Big Business could make it habitable for settlers from the USA. Plans went ahead: by 1911 the railway to Kennecott was open and the first gondolas rolled the 195 miles to the coast, each with a load worth from 12 to 15 thousand dollars apiece.

Daniel Guggenheim – the partnership's strong man.

Simon Guggenheim – the family's sole politician.

Simon was the only brother in politics. As Viceroy of the Guggenheim Empire in the West, he lived in Denver with a beautiful and clever wife, Olga Hirsch. He was a sad-eyed and shy man; at 29 he put himself up for Lt Governorship of Colorado, only to be disbarred for being too young. In 1898 he ran for Governor, but this campaign was farcical, tragic and corrupt. At least one Guggenheimite was shot dead by a rival faction, and the older brothers in New York made him withdraw. In 1906 he ran for the Senate and won. He had greased his electoral machine to run smoothly this time, though there was still a hullaballoo against him: "Simon Guggenheim in the U.S. Senate will be a joke and a most discreditable joke on Colorado." But on the whole he was popular and deserved to win. He did not use his position to lobby against popular causes and further mining interests. He did obstruct Pinchot's work in Alaska, but no resident of Colorado ever complained of his treatment of them. None was "too poor or obscure to receive the same courtesy".

112   Popular discontent grew with the Guggenheims'

fortune. In 1905 their offices (and those of Jakob Schiff) were bombed. But Dan steered his organisation with remarkable skill, always retaining his sense of proportion and his ability to see the other view. His daughter Gladys Straus quotes him: "If you knew the other feller's troubles, you'd keep your own." He insisted his employees didn't keep office boys waiting: "Their time is as valuable to them as mine is to me." One incident was particularly stylish. On Lafayette Street his car knocked down the boy of poor Italian immigrants. Dan faced an ugly crowd, took the boy in his arms, commanded a policeman to follow, and rushed to hospital. He waited till the parents were found, commiserated with them, paid the bills and more, and helped the family in various ways. The moment he got wind of the San Francisco Earthquake, he sent $50,000 with instructions: NO RED TAPE GIVE IT TO THE PEOPLE AT ONCE. Two carts, hauled by drays from Sausalito, went into the city and distributed the cash.

In 1907 the Guggenheims had their first real setbacks. A crisis of nerve on the stock market sliced the shares of the American Smelting and Refining Co. in two. It also made the brothers uneasy when John D. Rockfeller started buying them up. Then there was a disastrous episode over a mine called Nipissing, near Hudson Bay. Hammond recommended it. The Brothers agreed to buy for 10 million, with convenient, secret escape clauses. When the avid and sheepish stock market heard of their participation, Nipissing shares rocketed out of all proportion, since everything the Guggenheims touched was golden. Hammond's subordinate then reported that the vein of silver petered out at 20 feet. The Guggenheims dumped their shares and the bottom fell out. The ruined investors held them responsible, and said that Daniel had rigged the crash to discourage wild-cat speculation he couldn't control. Hammond retired, giving reasons of ill-health, only to write an obliquely worded article which hinted that the Nipissing crash *was* the Guggenheims' fault. Beatty had already left over a monumental row over the flotation of Yukon Gold, in which the Guggenheims accused him of getting the sellers to up the price with kickbacks for himself. In fact, the brothers were rather glad to be rid of their primadonna-ish employees; Daniel even referred to the cleaning of his Augean Stables. But the strain was beginning to tell. Isaac had a nervous breakdown and went to Switzerland, where doctors recommended him the treatment of Dr Weir Mitchell of Philadelphia. But Philadelphia, in this case, was too near home for the patient's good.

The mining industry was sick. Amorphous combines like the Smelters' Trust, with their omniscient blacklisting and total control, demoralised the workers and only asked for trouble. Solomon's insensitive remark: "I believe the wage earner is more extravagant in proportion to his earnings than the millionaire," showed that he, for one, was temporarily out of touch with reality. The Guggenheim's biographer Harvey O'Connor, himself a Socialist, said that smelting and mining had the reputation of being man-killers, and presented a picture of the industry as a torture chamber of crushed limbs and respiratory diseases. "As late as 1913," he wrote, "one man out of four in American smelting and refining plants suffered a disabling accident," the victims limping off to join the bands of wrecked and homeless men who tramped the skid-rows and hobo-jungles of America.

The years before the Great War were years of the International Workers of the World (the IWW or 'Wobblies'); of names like Gompers, Eugene Debs, and the 'one-eyed and two-fisted' Big Bill Haywood; and of the Ludlow Massacre, when guards of the Rockefellers' Colorado Fuel and Iron Co. burned to

death nineteen women and children in a camp of striking miners. In 1912 the Brothers sent the Wadell-Mahon strikebreakers into their refinery at Perth Amboy, New Jersey, whose smokestacks they could see from their office. Four men were shot. At Bingham Canyon there was a state of guerilla war. Dan Jackling, the manager, fortified by state troopers and the moral armour of Mormonism, ran it as a slave camp and short-circuited pressure from the Western Federation of Miners by importing cheap and bewildered Japanese, Slav, Greek and Hungarian miners, who knew no English and, he hoped, would not complain. This underestimated their intelligence and power of organisation. Furious workers paraded in Salt Lake City with placards: "Must we go to Russia for Feedom?" In the autumn of 1912, 6000 of them seized the mine and armed themselves with stolen rifles and nitro-glycerine, though they had left it too late in the year to hold out.

To their great credit, the Brothers heeded the warning signals. Encouraged by their attorneys Sam Untermeyer and Bernard Baruch, they hired Charles McNeill, the retiring U.S. Commissioner for Labour, to advise, and acted on his recommendations. Daniel was again wonderfully flexible. He volunteered to answer the questions of labour leaders, who sat on Woodrow Wilson's Industrial Relations Committee. His interrogators thought they had him cornered but he left them dumbfounded. He said that capitalists were often arbitrary; that he himself was 'socialistic'; that workers were quite justified in organising, and should not just have a voice but a *compelling* voice; and that the State must take over the burden of philanthropy, even if it meant taxing the estates of the rich.

War caught Daniel, unprepared and without money, at Baden-Baden, taking his annual cure. His son Harry Frank cabled him funds with the comment: "Now you know what it feels like to be broke." But the Brothers were far from broke, and were soon to be as rich as any other family in the United States or anywhere else. They controlled the world price of copper and the Allies needed every ounce of copper they could get. In one eight-month period Guggenheim enterprises shipped 234 million dollars worth of copper to England and France alone. Kennecott was returning fantastic dividends. In the U.S. they had the Ray, Nevada and Utah Copper Companies; they had mines in Mexico, the Braden mine in Chile. And now the greatest mine in the world had come their way: Chuquicamata, where 300 million tons of good ore lay close to the surface, 9000ft. up in the Chilean Andes. By March 1915 it had swung into

production.

Dan knew that the War would result in the ascendancy of the United States over Europe. He lobbied the government to get off the backs of the big companies and allow them full advantage over their crippled competitors. Isaac was even more cold-blooded: "I will say that the longer the war continues in Europe, the better it will be for us. In a short time the trouble abroad will make the U.S. the money centre of the world and we are certain to become a creditor instead of a debtor nation."

Yet the War caught the New York Jews in an anomalous position. It is true they had suddenly blossomed. The appalling Mrs Astor was dead. The Social Register already counted for less. Jewish bankers like Otto Kahn were positively fashionable and were exposing the provincial backwardness of the gentile crust. Jews set the pace for artistic New York, with their collections and benefactions to museums, opera and music. Daniel and Florence underwrote the popular Goldman concerts in Central Park. But the Jewish plutocracy was suspected of favouring Germany in the war, or actively helping the Bolsheviks undermine the Tsar. Some of the anti-Jewish feeling rubbed off on the Guggenheims. Once the U.S. entered the War, they found themselves pilloried as profiteers. Woodrow Wilson expected the big metal producers to be patriotic and lower their prices, but the Guggenheims (as well as Anaconda Mining) argued that the laws of supply and demand must apply even in war. Only when Wilson threatened nationalisation did the copper kings compromise and agree to peg the price at 23·5 cents a pound, when it could have gone well over 30; the pre-war price had been 14 or 15.

Meanwhile the Brothers had another dose of domestic trouble, from Will. By 1913 his income had dwindled below his life-style. Though he signed waivers whenever the Guggenheims began a new project, he felt they had misled him over the prospects of Chuquicamata. He brought an ugly lawsuit which they settled out of court for a rumoured five million when his attorney threatened to subpoena their account books. Throughout the war Will was hysterically anti-German and advocated total destruction. He said that German agents had been buying up all the black walnut trees for gunstocks and aircraft propellors. He asked patriots to hand in their Baedekers for Army officers to use. After the war he got even crankier. He died in 1941, leaving his money to Miss America of 1929 and Miss Connecticut of 1930, neither of whom, when the taxes were paid, collected more than a measly sum.

Harry with the rocket pioneer Robert Goddard and Charles Lindbergh at Goddard's launching site, 1935. Opposite: Harry going into action off Okinawa, 1945.

Elbcron no longer satisfied the Brothers' aspirations and they moved en bloc to large estates on the North Shore of Long Island. Dan bought a barracks of a house, called Castle Gould, built for the railroad king in a lugubrious Jacobean style. He renamed it Hempstead House, filled it with exotic plants and bought a Rembrandt. He sold his town house and moved to a suite in the St Regis Hotel. In 1919 he announced his retirement from business, but it was a busy retirement. With peace, copper slumped again to 15 cents, with no demand in the U.S. and no money in Europe. During one six-month period no copper was sold on the international market. There were lay-offs, mine-closures and unrest, and a government committee to investigate the indecent profits of the war. Henry Ford, at this time, launched his anti-Jewish campaign and published *Protocols of the Elders of Zion* in his newspaper, the *Dearborn Independent*. He also asserted that the man who made factories (like himself) owned them, whereas mine-exploiters (like the Guggenheims) were profiting from property that belonged to all. Worst of all, the directors of the American Smelting and Refining Company rebelled. They said the Guggenheims held insufficient shares to warrant their dictatorial behaviour and had milked the company dry. A stock-

115

(NY5) NEW YORK, July 24--GUGGENHEIM WITH TWO
THE FAMOUS COPPER FAMILY, WHO DIED LAST MONT
FORMER SHOW GIRLS TO WHOM HE LEFT HIS ESTATE
RIGHT, WITH MILDRED BORST. THE WILL WAS FIL
THE ESTATE'S ESTIMATED $1,000,000 VALUE WOUL

S NAMED IN WILL--WILLIAM GUGGENHEIM OF
72, IS SHOWN HERE WITH TWO OF THE FOUR
FT: GUGGENHEIM WITH MARY ALICE RICE;
STERDAY, BUT THERE WAS NO ASSURANCE THAT
ND UP. (AP WIREPHOTO) (JB51105MIR) 1941

holders' inquiry revealed that the Guggenheims and Whitneys, who once owned over half the stock, had in fact whittled their holdings down to under 10 per cent. and at the general meeting of 1922 the Brothers lost control of the company.

Disenchanted with metal, the Guggenheims expanded into raw nitrates, which, as a source of fertiliser and iodine and the essential ingredient of munitions, appeared to have a limitless future. Daniel was obsessed with nitrate. He told his family: "Nitrates will make us rich beyond the dreams of avarice." In partnership with the Chilean Government, their Anglo-Lautaro Nitrate Company bought out all but 2 per cent. of the nitrate in Chile, and controlled 85 per cent. of the world's production. But it chalked up millions in development costs, and the whole scheme went sour when, in 1929, a German discovered a process for making synthetic nitrate.

The family paid for this folly by losing their prize asset, Chuquicamata, sold in 1922 for $75,000,000 to Anaconda Mining, who ran it till its nationalisation by Allende. Isaac was the only brother to object to the sale, but he died at the critical moment, on holiday in England, at Southampton. Two members of the third generation also objected, Harry Frank

118 **Robert Guggenheim with third wife Elizabeth Eaton.**

and Edmond, the sons of Daniel and Murry. Both had worked in Chile and knew the slump was temporary. But Dan contravened Meyer's old principle of unanimity, railroaded the sale through, and, by refusing to listen to the young, destroyed the continuity of the partnership. Harry Frank turned to his love, the aeroplane, and Edmond to golf. And they were the only two Guggenheims who showed the least inclination to work.

The family was facing a demographic crisis. There were abundant Guggenheim heiresses, many of whom were unhappy about being Jewish; these tended to marry Englishmen, not all of whom were satisfactory. But there were few heirs. There was a sickly William Guggenheim II. Simon had two sons: one, John Simon, died of mastoid at 22; the other, George Denver, was also sick and shot himself in New York in 1939. A fellow-member of the Harvard Class of '29 remembers him as "all dressed up and nowhere to go".

The one other possibility was Daniel's other son, Meyer Robert, who disabused any illusions his father held for him. Early in life he announced: "Every family supports at least one gentleman of leisure. I have elected to assume that position in mine." He did serve in the War and was "the best damned general's aide in the U.S. Army", but thereafter devoted himself to racehorses, yachts, bull-terriers (which he slightly resembled) and several wives, changing his religion from the Jewish to Catholic to Lutheran to suit the next bride. In 1953 he was Eisenhower's Ambassador to Portugal and soon returned *persona non grata* after he had inserted a teaspoon down a lady's cleavage at a diplomatic dinner – and tried to rescue it. In 1959 the old soldier collapsed in a taxi in Georgetown, died, and was buried in Arlington National Cemetery. Afterwards the Federal Government claimed $169,543 taxes unpaid on gifts to an "unidentified lady friend" of cash, jewellery and a modest house – in Georgetown.

Another grandson of Meyer's was Harold, the son of Rose Guggenheim and Albert Loeb. Loeb is the athletic, unhappy New York Jew, who never quite makes it, whom Hemingway cruelly portrayed as Robert Cohn in *The Sun Also Rises*. Loeb did the rounds of Paris ateliers, knew Joyce, Fitzgerald, Hart Crane and William Carlos Williams, and pioneered in New York with an avant-garde magazine called *Broom*. His autobiography *The Way It Was*, gives his version of those bull-fighting episodes at Pamplona.

As their business sense declined the Brothers started their charitable foundations and discovered how to give their money away, without stinginess and with-

Daniel Guggenheim (sitting second from left) with prominent aviators, 1927. Orville Wright is on his left.

out wounding the *amour propre* of the receivers. Dan said: "The money must go back to the people." He set up two funds for aeronautical research. Feeling guilty perhaps about Chuquicamata, he acted on the advice of Harry, who had a kind of Nietzschean obsession with the aeroplane since his tennis partner at Cambridge had been killed flying. The post-war American aircraft industry was languishing for lack of enthusiasm and money. A conservative public baulked at the idea of a passenger airline. Dan's fund helped change that. It latched on to Lindbergh *after* he flew *The Spirit of St Louis* to Paris. Harry rescued the golden boy from the lionisers and settled him in his new mansion, Falaise, where he wrote *We*, his log of the flight. The fund financed Capt H. Doolittle's first unassisted landing in fog; a gyroscopic compass; a prize for the safest aircraft; a weather service for forecasting fog; and the first American airline, the Western Air Express. It set up chairs of aeronautical engineering in California, at MIT and other universities. It imported to the California Institute of Technology, the Hungarian aerospace engineer Theodor von Karman, the inventor of the wind tunnel and smooth flight. The first big success of the von Karman era was the Douglas DC-3.

Dan next poured funds into the last project one would associate with an ageing millionaire. Lindbergh and Harry had got wind of the experiments of Dr Robert H. Goddard, a Massachussets professor, who had attracted the derision of the Press with the 'moon rocket' he flew in his Aunt Effie's pasture. Neighbours complained of the fire risk; one lady said the Professor's radio waves had "pierced the apex of her heart". In fact Goddard was an unworldly, uncommunicative genius of the first rank, and had proved that rockets could propel themselves in a vacuum, that is, in outer space. "If we had a million dollars," he said, "we could send a rocket to the

Harry Guggenheim and his horse Dark Star, with which he won the Kentucky Derby in 1953.

moon, but where would we get a million dollars?"

Dan did not give a million, but enough for Goddard to move to New Mexico, where his rockets, all christened *Nell*, grew bigger and rose higher, to 10,000ft. Dan was fascinated, and before he died told Gladys Straus: "I'm not going to live to see it, but you'll live to see the mail shot over to Europe." Goddard always got a lukewarm reception from the U.S. armed forces; but other eyes were fixed on his experiments. When, finally, the Pentagon sent a captured German V-2 rocket to Annapolis, Goddard and his assistant were summoned to inspect its insides. "Looks like our Nell," said the assistant. "Seems to be," Goddard said. After the war, with ironic justice the U.S. Government incarcerated the captured Nazi rocket and bomb experts in Dan's Hempstead House and put them to work.

Solomon was a stubborn man, and Dan's ulcer was said to be "Solomon-caused". He was an Anglo-

phile, and two of his daughters married Englishmen: one of them, Eleanor, is the present Viscountess Castle Stewart. He was kind but cool to his wife Irene, kept mistresses and would pronounce on their care and feeding. In 1926 he was 65 and not taking kindly to old age when he received the visit of the red-haired and blue-eyed abstract painter Baroness Hilla von Rebay, the daughter of a Prussian general. The Baroness later described her affair as a sexless relationship, but, if so, it was not in keeping with Solomon's character. She plunged him into the European avant garde, took him to the Bauhaus, made him buy a marvellous collection of paintings by Kandinsky, Klee, Moholy-Nagy and other, mainly non-objective, artists, and encouraged him to open his own museum.

The Baroness did have one monumental lapse of judgment – her enthusiasm for the work of her one great love, the Polish painter, Rudolf Bauer, a plagiariser – and later patroniser – of Kandinsky. The Baroness made Solomon buy Bauers in bulk. When the painter fell foul of the Nazis, she shipped him to New Jersey, where he promptly married his housekeeper. She soon got entangled in a libel suit with the new Frau Bauer, a case not even the Guggenheims' attorney would touch. When the U.S. entered the War, Bauer hit back and denounced the Baroness as a Nazi agent who was provisioning enemy submarines.

The Solomon Guggenheim Museum of Non-Objective Art had opened in 1939 with the Baroness as director. She dismissed Picasso and Dada, and said Surrealism was "inartistic kitsch". The great master (in 1939) was Bauer – Max Ernst called the Museum the Bauer-House. The tipsy prose of the Baroness's publications was a standing joke:

> "Mr Guggenheim whose life work consists in revealing and opening up the hidden wealth of the earth is a leader of the mining industry. Sometimes, in spite of discouragements, he continues his vocation to lead with the same intuitive foresight that attracted him to other fields: namely the ethereal spirit of art as a counterbalance to earth."

The art critics smelled blood. The museum, they said, was a tax-exempt institution and should pursue a less partisan policy. The director should not swamp exhibitions with her own paintings and those of her "once close friend". One venomous columnist suggested that the paintings should be handed over to some properly-run institution.

But the Baroness had real qualities and Solomon stuck by her. He hired Frank Lloyd Wright to design "something unusual" to house the collection, cried when shown the model, and said: "Mr Wright. This is it." He never saw the upward-spiralling ramp on Fifth Avenue, and missed the memorable rows that swirled round the head of his Trustee, Harry Frank. Robert Moses, the New York Parks Commissioner, said the building was "like an inverted cup and saucer with a silo added for luck", and hoped it could be squeezed into "some not-too-conspicuous corner of a suburban park". The architect himself, a self-advertised genius of the order of Michelangelo, hinted that the museum would only be perfect *without* the Guggenheim collection. When the new director, James Johnson Sweeney, wanted to paint it white inside, Wright said it would look like the "toilets of the Racquet Club". The Baroness said it was a pigsty. But when, finally, it opened in 1962, the public was enchanted.

Two other Guggenheims set up foundations. The least known was Murry's (now extinct) free dental clinic for the New York poor. The best known is the John Simon Guggenheim Foundation, which Senator Simon gave in memory of his dead son. Simon's idea was to buy a sabbatical year for artists, writers and scientists – not in the U.S. alone, but in all American countries, since the Guggenheims made their money in Latin America. To run it Simon employed a brilliant talent scout, Henry Allen Moe. The underlying idea is that real achievement is born in solitude. The Foundation gives no money to groups, only to individuals (who are also cheaper). Unlike other foundations, the Guggenheim attaches no strings, demands no pound of flesh. If the receiver wants to contemplate his navel for a year, he is welcome to do so. After 50 years the Foundation is still, perhaps, the most inspired piece of philanthropy in America.

But *the* Guggenheim phenomenon is Ben's daughter Peggy. She was never ashamed of being Jewish, and has always actively thrived on chaos. She had less money than her name suggested to the spongers and made more than she inherited. As a girl she escaped from the Guggenheim orbit and lived in Europe, where she was often unhappy, longing to be loved but usually looking cheerful. She had love affairs with a professional bohemian, Laurence Vail; with an English writer manqué John Holmes; with an English Marxist intellectual; with Samuel Beckett. Then she discovered her prodigious talent – the collecting of art and artists. She collected Brancusi and Tanguy in both senses; she started the Guggenheim-Jeune Gallery in London, to the fury of Solomon's Baroness; she planned a proper Museum of Modern Art in London, since the Tate Gallery was beyond hope, but the scheme fell through. At the fall of France she bought a wonderful collection of modern pictures, and escaped to the United States with them and Max Ernst, whom she briefly married. She took up with Jackson Pollock and artfully put him under contract to deliver her his entire production. This he did not do, and Peggy spent years in litigation with the artist's widow. After the war she moved to Venice, to the *Palazzo Venier dei Leoni*, where she and her collection are among the city's enduring monuments. She has left her house and collection to her Uncle Solomon's museum, on condition it remains in Venice "even if Venice sinks".

The desks of the Guggenheim Brothers still line the partners' office at 120 Lower Broadway, but the staff is small and there is not much activity. The head of the family is now Peter Lawson-Johnston, a grandson of Solomon and Harry's heir. He is an energetic man in his late forties, whose job is to pick up the bits of the fallen Guggenheim Empire.

The Bauhaus, 1929: Solomon Guggenheim (right) with his wife Irene, Vasily Kandinsky and Hilla von Rebay.

All his life Harry Guggenheim pretended to enjoy the great wealth that had imploded on him. Whatever he did he did well. He won the Kentucky Derby in 1953 with Dark Star, but his standards were those of the dilettante. He could have had a career in aviation, and was hailed as one of its pioneers, but he threw that talent away. In 1929 he was Ambassador to Cuba and had a rather doubtful friendship with the dictator of the day, the bloodthirsty General Machado y Morales. The truth is, he was flawed, incomplete, obsessed with fantasies of heroism, leadership and power, and brought great unhappiness to whoever crossed his path. His third wife, Alicia Patterson, was a brilliant newspaper-woman, for whom he started the Long Island daily, *Newsday*. She was a liberal and a Democrat. His politics had crystallised into a harsh Republicanism. She won for *Newsday* the Pulitzer Prize for journalism, but he kept 51 per cent. of the shares, knowing she would leave him if he gave her 2 per cent. more. When she died, miserable and exhausted, Harry assumed the editorship and set about erasing her influence. Finally he sold *Newsday* to a reactionary Californian chain.

* * * * *

Despite their appetite for accumulation, the original Guggenheim brothers had a humorous diffidence about their wealth. They realised they were playing that risky game, so close to the source of Jewish persistence, in which money means communication and vitality. Harry Frank had lost their talent and their optimism. He was closer to the concept that property is the seat of power. For years he brooded over his will and judged his daughters and grandchildren unworthy. With his friend Charles Lindbergh he got interested in Neo-Darwinian studies of animal behaviour that seemed to condone an ideology of force, "the drive", as he put it, "of any person in human society to control, direct or coerce, or manipulate another or others, for ends devised by the dominator". He discussed his ideas with the writer Robert Ardrey. And he conceived a new Guggenheim Foundation, utterly devoid of the Liberal idealism of his uncle's, to explore patterns of social dominance in man. He called it 'Man's Relation to Man' and presided over the first meeting, ironically, in the old house of Henry Ford, at Dearborn, now part of the University of Michigan. On his death in 1971, the Harry Guggenheim Foundation triumphed over the interests of the family, and now runs with a working capital of $18 million, with more assets to come in. It is, I believe, the first of its kind in America, and would surely have horrified the Brothers. In its published report, one of the recipients, Professor Sherwood Washburn suggests that the social systems of animals and humans will not work without violence, and that individuals must get hurt. The other projects echo the same line and suggest that Harry's money, allied to this kind of research, questions the value of both.

123

ROOSEVELT

Peter Conrad

Opposite: Theodore Roosevelt after the attempt on his life in Milwaukee, October 1912.

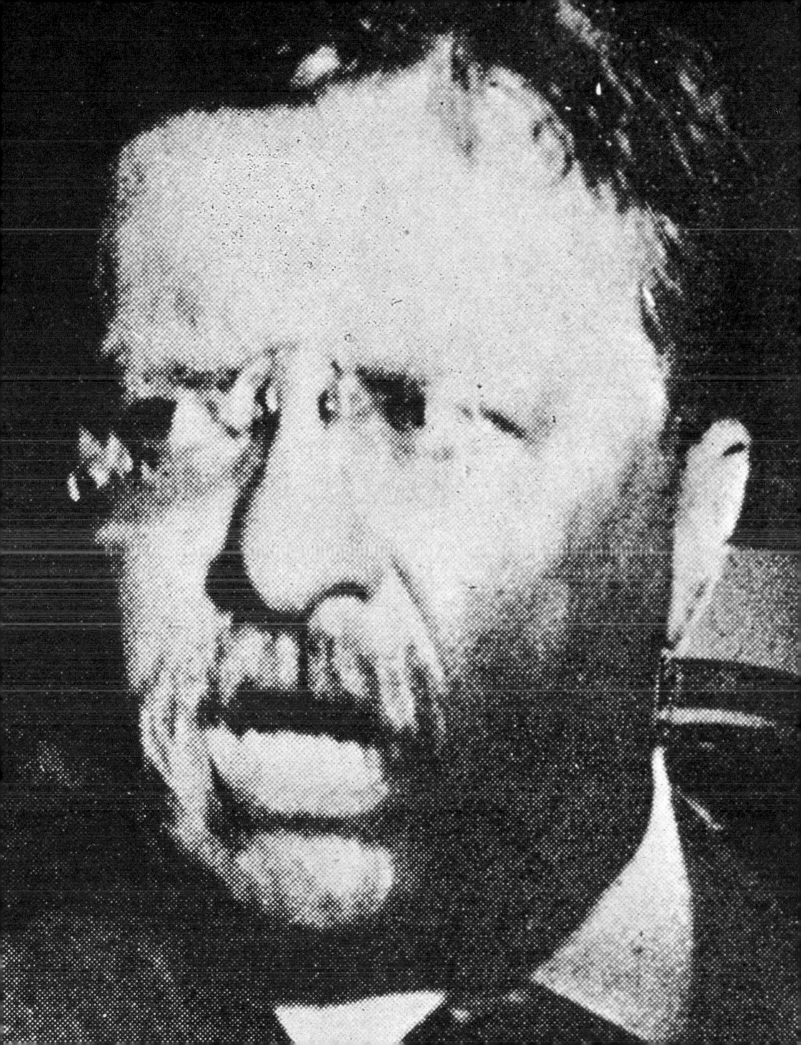

Teddy Roosevelt as he liked to be seen – the outdoor sportsman.

As a dynasty the Roosevelts fit together oddly, almost accidentally. The connections of kin are tenuous and indirect, and although the family supplied two presidents within half a century they were of opposite political persuasions, and the vital link between them depends, matriarchally, on a woman. Eleanor Roosevelt, Theodore's niece and Franklin's fifth cousin, turns out to be the central figure, and the family's true history consists not in its presidential successes but in her emergence as the unelected conscience of the world.

In a cartoon published by *Vanity Fair* in 1933, Miguel Covarrubias devised an 'impossible interview' between the two Presidents as jubilant fireworks exploded over the White House. Theodore, his square Dutch block-shaped head a ghostly verdigris, his paw clasping a gnarled club, glowers at a harassed, wrinkled, pink Franklin, who has only his walking stick for a weapon. Theodore expresses his dismay at hearing about the New Deal, which will give "the old boys the gate"; Franklin reassures him and asks why his ghost is troubling the grounds. Theodore says plaintively, "I'd like to win a place in history too – as the fifth cousin of a famous man." The meeting seems to occur across a gulf of time, as Theodore's glum sense of his own obsolescence acknowledges. They belong in quite different worlds. Theodore expresses the late 19th century's elation of power; he seems always to be photographed astride things: camels, bucking broncoes, buffaloes or flying machines. His attitude is one of confident possession, standing with portly smugness in his White House office leaning on a globe, or mounted on a steam shovel, or swathed in oilskins on a submarine, or portentously installed behind the lectern in the Sheldonian Theatre delivering the Romanes lecture. In contrast with this hero of bulk and assertive swagger, Franklin belongs in the maladies and crises of the 20th century, coping from his wheel-chair with the spontaneous combustion of capitalism. And yet it is only a quirk of family history which prevents their being contemporaries: they belong in the same generation. Theodore was fifth in line of descent from Johannes Roosevelt, born in 1689; Franklin was five generations removed from the brother of Johannes, Jacobus, born in 1692. The biblical tedium of the genealogy was disrupted by Franklin's father, who remarried in middle age and so placed Franklin incongruously a generation later than Theodore. Instead of a dynasty remorselessly passing on an inherited weight of wealth and power, the Roosevelts are an informal triangle of cousins from different branches of the same family. Giving her away at her wedding, Theodore complimented Eleanor on her neatness in choosing another Roosevelt.

The family is an intriguing self-contradiction: a dynasty only by chance, and a dynasty of politicians which remains dear to Americans because it seems to represent an apology for politics. The idea of politics – of the need for lubricating bribes and covert deals to adjust opposed interests, of a profession in which duplicity is an essential qualification – has always offended Americans, who cherish the faith that interests will reconcile themselves automatically, as discordant races will be melted down into a uniform stew in the pot. In the democratic paradise Americans hoped to create, politics would be irrelevant, since the duty of happiness is enjoined on every citizen, and politics is the morbid area of grievance, disgruntlement and self-tormenting public ambition which contradicts the private contentment central to America's pastoral idea of itself.

The presidency was invented to abolish politics. The process of election is a kind of transubstantiation, an election in the Calvinist sense – not a political contest but an assurance of entry into grace. A candidate who emerges to bargain for sectional interests must, once elected, generalise himself into the father of all; a politician must translate himself into a deity. In practice most holders of the office have contrived to play at sanctity in their various ways – Franklin Roosevelt by exhuming for his own uses the idea of a liberating Lincoln, Truman folksily, Eisenhower by affecting a military superiority to political calculation, Kennedy by risking himself and national security with a heroism Schlesinger thought chivalric and Mailer existential – while occupying themselves privately with the grimy business of government. The puritan conscience, employing hypocrisy to sustain the pretence of innocence, has seen to it to cover the gap. Nixon's crime was to be so brazenly political, so professionally tricky and ingenious, to resist the camouflage of an image. He tried to provide himself with one in his book *Six Crises*, portraying those occasions when his own network of deals and evasions trapped him as soul-forging trials, but once ensconced in the presidency he abandoned the claim to noble feeling and set about ruling technologically, through an intermediary army of gadgets and a poetic diction forged for his henchmen in order to help them obscure embarrassing truths. Nixon was too serious a politician to be an acceptable president; his constituents were as shocked by his craft as we should be if the Queen betrayed some animating tremor of intelligence and acquired a third dimension. This is perhaps why so many presidents have been assassinated: nothing in Kennedy's political career became him like the leaving of it; assassination at least confers

The rugged face of Teddy Roosevelt. Top: the officer, Spanish-American War, 1898. Above: the Harvard athlete. Left: the hunter with his kill. 129

on the politician who may not have earned sanctity the melancholy status of martyr. The demented ladies in California who aimed guns at Gerald Ford were trying to do him a favour: blissfully ordinary as he is, they were trying to wish an extraordinary fate on him. Assassination was for them, as for Manson's accomplices in the assault on Sharon Tate's house, a high moral duty. Not even that sanction would have worked against Nixon, whose worst failing in American eyes is his resilience, his rational and unheroic refusal to accept the disabilities of honour and death.

Theodore Roosevelt apologised for politics by translating it into sport; Franklin and Eleanor translated it into philanthropy. None of them ever confessed to an interest in the disposition of power. For Theodore, power was dissipated in play, either in killing wild beasts or romping with infants; for Franklin and Eleanor, power modestly converted itself into service. Theodore's reminiscences of his hunting trips or his letters to his infantile friends are parables disowning power. The hunting trips treat power as a training in manly vigour, while the letters mask it in the jovial ritual of a game. English hunting has a comical gratuitousness: as Oscar Wilde said, the unspeakable pursue the uneatable; what matters is the society of the chase not the victory over the quarry. Like the Wife of Bath on the Canterbury pilgrimage, most members of an English hunting party complacently go along for the ride. Americans stalk their prey more earnestly and confront it alone: Theodore the wild game hunter or Hemingway's bullfighters or Faulkner's bear hunter, or the gunfighter at noon in the empty dusty Western street, or the detective edging his way down the perilous tracks of an urban jungle, are American images of the individual freed from the solemn hypocrisy of the community to enjoy the violent self-jeopardising exhilaration of power. Turning politics into sport excuses it by presenting it as healthy athleticism but also confesses its secret aggressiveness: the diplomat walking softly and carrying a big stick becomes the hunter walking softly and carrying a big gun. Thus Theodore's wolf hunting in Texas or grizzly bear slaying in Louisiana and Mississippi or rhino slaying in the Wakamba country are not innocent diversions but ferocious campaign trips: the beasts are his subjects, eagerly surrendering their lives to him. The safari park is an autocrat's dream of a political constituency. "In Yellowstone the animals seem always to behave as one wishes them to!" Theodore marvelled. The politician persuades and intrigues to make people behave as he wishes them to; the hunter gets the same result more speedily by aiming his gun.

Theodore's heroism is not existential, as Mailer took Kennedy's to be, but pugilistic and martial. His essays meditate on the tradition which connects him with the epic feats of Siegfried slaying the dragon or the romance prodigies of Charlemagne chasing the bison. A favourite artist of his, Frederic Remington, had made the same ennobling connections in *The Last Cavalier* in 1895, in which a cocky cow-puncher rides towards his apotheosis in the shadowy company

Teddy Roosevelt (centre) with hunting companions Wilmot Dow (on the left) and William Sewall, in 1884.

of horsemen who traverse the long centuries of Western history, from helmeted mediaeval knights to Stuart adventurers with feathers trailing from their hats. The cowboy has become a spiritual athlete, not a gun-toting tough but a knight of faith and an exemplar of the strenuous life.

Hunting was a ferocious compensation for, and juvenile games a guileless redemption of, politics. Theodore disburdened himself of the cares of office by romping with young constituents who "persist in regarding me as a playmate". Politics are therapeutically worked off in play, though Theodore's residual adult conscience was sometimes pained by this sort of inanity: "really it seems, to put it mildly, rather odd for a stout, elderly President to be bouncing over hay-ricks in a wild effort to get to goal before an

131

active midget of a competitor, aged nine years. However, it was really great fun." It had always been an American pretence that the president is merely the common man raised to a Platonic idea of himself. Because the presidency is a fantasy, it is therefore democratically available to anyone who can daydream: Franklin Roosevelt once said to a friend, "Wouldn't you be President if you could? Wouldn't anybody?", as if wishing could make it so. In America, stardom can be achieved in the absence of talent, and the presidency in the absence of qualification. Although presidents regularly pass themselves off as common men, Theodore was unique in wanting to ingratiate with children; Cecil Spring-Rice, the British Ambassador, remarked in a letter that "you must always remember that the President is about six". Play was not entirely the expense of spirit in a waste of inconsequence, however; it was also indoctrination. Theodore presided over the antics benevolently, "touched by the way in which [the children] feel that I am their special friend, champion, and companion", and their tennis games became a lisping mimicry of the political process in which the president acts as arbiter, distributing rewards to those whom economic competition declares as victors: "I officiated as umpire and furnished the prizes, which were penknives." Recent presidents have distributed ball-point pens to the crowds acclaiming them, as if handing out indulgences or plastic splinters of the true cross; a litter of cheap gifts solemnises and sentimentalises their relationship

Teddy Roosevelt on a crane at the Panama Canal construction site. Opposite: the family man – his daughter Alice stands at the back of the group. Following page: the Roosevelt home at Sagamore Hill, Long Island.

with the voters.

Theodore made politics a romp, an outdoor adventure; Franklin with his fireside chats on the radio, Eleanor with her Sunday teas on NBC television, serving distinguished guests from a silver urn with simulated casualness, brought politics back indoors. Theodore's Darwinian enthusiasm for strenuous exertion and the morality of muscle ("I do not like to see young Christians with shoulders that slope like a champagne bottle," he said) softened in the next generation into a concern for social casualties, a compassion for the unfit. Franklin and Eleanor domesticated politics. Hospitality was the answer they proposed to social problems – in her early days in New York whenever a beggar importuned Eleanor she brought him back home to eat at her table, and she professed to regret that she couldn't do the same at the White House; Franklin addressed his subjects as "my friends", cajoling them into a sense of personal obligation to him, inciting them to acts of superfluous generosity – during the period of the gold policy the White House was besieged by a miscellany of tributary offerings, a gold tooth, a wedding ring, even a pair of gold spectacles from a doting lady who said: "I'm getting too old to read much anyway." These sacrifices were sadly beside the point, but Americans long to believe that economic and social destinies can be magically transformed by effusions of goodwill, and Franklin encouraged them in the misapprehension. He scaled down his imperial office to that of a provincial constable, intervening in the gossipy disputes of the locals – a farmer's wife from the mid-West wrote to him, "Dear Frank: Our neighbour, Pete Smith, loaned us $25 on our team. He says he'll take the mules unless he can come to see me when my husband is away. How can I save the mules?"

Whereas Theodore had found an analogy for politics in the hunt and "the brotherhood of rifle, horse, and hound", Franklin was less of a predator and, once confined to his wheel-chair and deprived of the consolation of action, treated politics as a game of skill. The analogy which suits his style is cards; it occurs throughout Compton Mackenzie's biography of him. His preferred game was piquet, and Mackenzie describes his political career as "masterly piquet play", since the piquet player bluffingly makes his winning hand seem the result merely of luck. Manoeuvring for position in Woodrow Wilson's administration, Franklin employed the wily prevarication of the piquet player: tempted by the offer of Collector of the Port of New York and then by that of Assistant Secretary of the Treasury, he discarded both aces, as Mackenzie puts it, and having established his point

was automatically invited to become Assistant Secretary of the Navy. Mackenzie even belabours the card-playing conceit lurking in the catch-phrase "the New Deal", which was indeed an opportunistically gambling series of guesses not a systematic imposition of Socialism: "The New Deal had been dealt. Of the President's hand one could say that he had discarded the rich men's clubs and the diamonds of Wall Street, had established an overwhelming point in spades with a septième to the ace of agriculture, picked up a quint-major in hearts from his countrymen, piqued his opponents, and taken every trick from Congress in a capot that could be laid on the table." There may be too much of the clubman's leisured urbanity to Mackenzie's notion of the game, and, just as Theodore had seen life as a metaphysical football-game in which the imperative rule was "Hit the line hard; don't foul and don't shirk, but hit the line hard!", so Franklin himself favoured an analogy from football. In an early Press conference he likened himself to a quarterback who can predict the next play but nothing beyond it and so is unable to plan, as "future plays will depend on how the next one works". The New Deal was chancily improvisatory not dogmatic: the games Franklin played were games requiring tactical skill, games of experimental and haphazard adjustment; Theodore's games required merely the constitution of a bull-moose, which he boasted of possessing, and the psychology of a mutt, which one of his own Bull-Moose chieftains credited him with.

Theodore's fate was to earn immortality as a cuddly toy, the Teddy Bear; and Eleanor, whose daughter Anna wrote a book called *Scamper, the Bunny Who Went to the White House*, also regarded it as part of her duty to suffer little children. She narrated Prokofiev's *Peter and the Wolf* with Koussevitzky at Tanglewood, and each year recited Kipling stories to parties of slum schoolchildren who picnicked at Hyde Park. America has a blithe knack of taking romanticism literally, and one of the romantic myths its social life has unquestioningly institutionalised is the belief that the child is the father of the man. A metaphor has been turned into a fact. The child in America is conceded moral priority; all social occasions revolve around his querulous presence, and the culture and the gastronomy of the country are organised so as to 133

convince him never to grow up or console him for having done so. Theodore's homilies democratise the mystic wisdom of Wordsworth's ode: "the boy can best become a good man by being a good boy – not a goody-goody boy, but just a plain good boy", the sentence choking on its own smarmy self-repetition. It is claimed, apocryphally it seems, that a letter sent to Franklin which began, "Dear Mr President: You are the child of destiny" was directed to the Children's Bureau of the White House by a mail-sorting clerk. The error has its peculiar aptness: Franklin was the child of destiny but also the father of his people, for Gore Vidal has remarked in his novel *Two Sisters* that "believing in a man, taking seriously a President, is to enjoy the security of childhood come a second time". The genius, Baudelaire said, is one who can recover childhood at will; the American exists permanently in this fortunate state. All Americans took the shock of Nixon's treachery personally because it made them admit the untrustworthiness of the father, and expelled them from their complacent nursery.

The American political leader is obliged to assume the parental task of explaining life to his unfledged dependants, and the Roosevelts did so with self-righteous gusto. Eleanor said that the president "is, or ought to be, the great educator of the people". Theodore dramatised his political career as a pilgrim's progress, a Faustian agitation towards a goal which recedes into the elusive distance: "Life is a long campaign, where every victory merely leaves the ground free for another battle, and sooner or later defeat comes to every man, unless death forestalls it". The mischances of political fortune become movements of the wheel of destiny; success becomes an emblem of spiritual triumph and defeat a reminder of mortal limitation. Life is promoted to a 'Great Adventure'.

For Anglo-Saxons, this is one of the philosophical puzzles of America – just as the Germans refuse to trust to the prosaic substance of a thing, to take it on its own terms as we pragmatically do, but must translate it into an idea, so Americans refuse to accept the belittling circumstances which enclose us all, and must transfigure their existences by arriving at a radiant concept of themselves. The Germans intellectualise, the Americans idealise. Their society is urged on towards a self-glorifying image of itself as a 'Great Society'; their own membership of it is not something to be compliantly enjoyed, a natural rootedness which it would be unnatural to think about, but a gift of grace to be marvelled at and cherished, because it can be taken away. Hence the

PHOTOGRAPH BY WM DINWIDDIE
COPYRIGHTED

use of the word 'American' as an honorary title rather than a non-committal label. Addressing the Hamilton Club in Chicago in 1899, Theodore rallied the members as "men of the State which gave to the country Lincoln and Grant, men who pre-eminently and distinctly embody all that is most American in the American character". To be American is to belong to a category of spirit, not just to possess a passport:

Teddy Roosevelt's private army, the Rough Riders, 1898.

Theodore proclaimed this notion of citizenship as a stigmatising mark of favour not a natural right in saying that "Americanism is a question of spirit, conviction, and purpose, not of creed or birthplace". The House Committee on Un-American Activities based an inquisition on this sense of Americanism as a privilege not a birthright.

In the same way, life for Americans cannot remain a fact but must become a value; it is not enough supinely to live: one's life must become an allegory. Theodore achieved the feat of self-allegorising by making himself a bull-moose galloping across a landscape in pursuit, like Tennyson's Ulysses, of a fading ideal; Eleanor achieved it not by heroic example but by homiletic instruction. Her manuals of

137

homely advice, one of which is called *You Learn by Living*, assume that living is not a natural talent like breathing but something to be painfully acquired, like reading, and the presumption reveals much about the American character. Because life is somehow not a value in the United States, where nothing is real because not validated and authorised by time, where all arrangements and constructions are temporary and all people constantly mobile, Americans feel a nagging need to awaken themselves into life. Life is not what they are, but what they might hopefully become. Lam-

bert Strether in Henry James's *The Ambassadors* tells little Bilham to "live". Coming from a character of another nationality, the advice would seem absurdly trite: is not little Bilham alive already? Delivered by an American, it becomes positively messianic. Hence the importance of Eleanor's tracts, which democratise the romantic sense of wonder, making the genius Baudelaire thought so rare available effortlessly to all. She enforces a naïve omnivorousness, insisting *"You must be interested in anything that comes your way"*, communalising the romantic intuition of uniqueness

Teddy Roosevelt on the election trail: campaigning for Vice-President on William McKinley's ticket in 1900.

and so transforming it from a means of self-discovery and mental independence into a technique for social adjustment: "Since everybody is an individual, nobody can be you . . . Your life is your own. You make it." A society which has abolished history, as America Adamically prided itself on doing, abolishes parents too: all Americans are children because they confront their brave new world together, untainted by custom and inheritances of habit. They cannot be disabused by Prospero's nasty slur: it is indeed new to them. But needing a tribal leader, they elect a president to act as their collective parent, and since there is no tradition of moral lore to guide them, he must tell them everything, including how to live, which they can't just automatically and insentiently do. Theodore rigged up commandments from the boy scout's code: "be a good man to camp out with", he said; Eleanor's wisdom was hastily fabricated in answer to queries sent to her at the *Ladies Home Journal*, in which she was catechistically sentententious about trivia: no, she

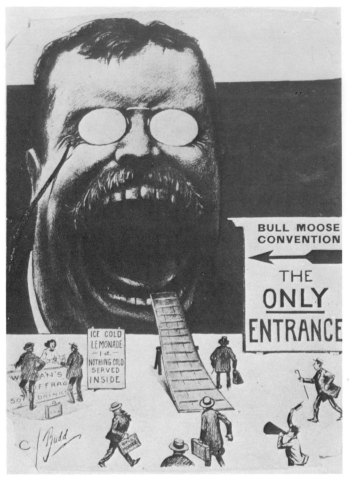

Teddy Roosevelt as the target of cartoonists over his for

Text within image: ...ING AT NATIONAL NEGRO BUSINESS LEAGUE COPYRIGHT 1910 BY GEO G. BAIN BOOKER T. WASHINGTON.

...cies (left) and his breakaway 'Bull Moose' Party (top left). Above: addressing a meeting of the Negro Business League.

The attempt on Teddy Roosevelt in Milwaukee, 1912: John Schrank's revolver.

was not superstitious, but sometimes she knocked on wood; yes, she preferred classical music to 'hot' music, but only because she knew it better; yes, she believed children should be taught to believe in Santa Claus. Popular psychology carries on the Roosevelt tradition of amateur prophecy in contemporary America: Theodore's iron, enduring, self-reliant hero thrilled to the sense of his own manly health; the American of today no longer feels his uniqueness to be the dazzling blessing Eleanor proclaimed it, but psychology has taught him to take a lugubrious pleasure in noting the progress of his diseases.

Inside the same family, the change from one generation to the next represents a shift in conscience and sensibility. For Theodore civilisation was to be maintained by competitive virility, infusions of procreative energy: he declared it the racial duty of every able-bodied American male to beget an average of four children. For Franklin and Eleanor, civilisation consisted in kindly amelioration of the damage done by Theodore's ethic of brash striving. For Theodore, civilisation was a biological idea: he delivered the Romanes lecture at Oxford in 1910 on the subject of biological analogies in history, and warned against a

decline from martial alertness into soft luxury and vapid ease; his letters to children prickle with sour allegories about the decadence of over-indulgence: "Quentin's sickness was surely due to a riot in candy and ice-cream with chocolate sauce. He was a very sad bunny next morning." For Franklin and Eleanor, civilisation needed to redeem itself as a moral idea. Although Herbert Hoover found in the New Deal a scarifying advance of Socialism, Franklin was no doctrinaire tyrant but a man of social privilege whose nobility obliged him to succour his labouring inferiors. The emotion which bound the American working people to Franklin was not socialist solidarity but a gratitude they might feel towards an unexpectedly benevolent employer: a cartoon on the sports page of the New York *Journal* on Franklin's birthday in 1934 showed an undernourished family of rustics at a sparsely laid table toasting Franklin, whose beaming affluent visage floated in the air like a planet next to the stove-pipe.

Eleanor was more of a radical than he because for her the discovery of poverty and social distress was a personal horror. Her exposure to the gibbering indecencies of St Elizabeth's, the asylum for shell-

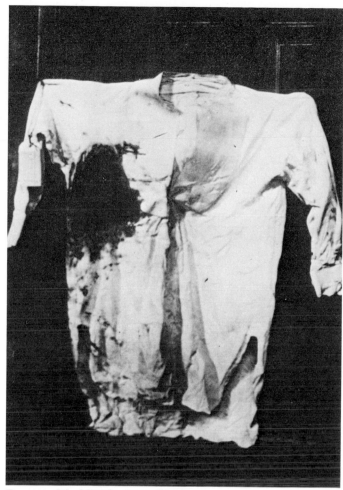

Roosevelt's blood-covered shirt.

John Schrank, would-be assassin.

shocked sailors and marines in which Ezra Pound was later incarcerated, was an equivocal awakening, like the discovery by the governess in *The Turn of the Screw* of the activities of salacious ghosts in closed rooms, or Adela Quested's nauseous vastation in the echoing cave in *A Passage to India*. Poverty embarrassed and shamed her; social reform was simply the most brisk and hygienic way to remove it from sight. Like sex, which she disliked, poverty was unwelcome evidence of human foulness. The connection between the two prohibited areas was made when a visitor garrulously referred to her "passionate interest" in welfare legislation; Eleanor firmly demurred: "I hardly think the word 'passionate' applies to me." Her testimony before a Congressional Committee catches the tone of alarmed disgust: "I came away with the feeling that if in the United States, Blue Plains was our conception of how to care for the aged we were at a pretty low ebb of civilisation. It was a sick feeling you got from the whole atmosphere."

Theodore apologised for politics by making it an arena for energy ("aggressive fighting for the right is the noblest sport the world affords"), Franklin and Eleanor by making it a field for the evangelism of conscience. Their retreat from power, resolving government into gymnastics on the one hand and charity on the other, goes with their pastoral disowning of their inheritance. Remarkable individuals, they felt obliged to divest themselves of this individuality and become humble scraps of humanity. The ideal is democratised in America as the inoffensive type: the Roosevelts boasted of their sublime ordinariness. A petty officer on the *Louisiana* proposed a toast to Theodore as "the typical American citizen!"; Franklin became the champion of the oppressed average, symbolising Norman Rockwell's *Century of the Common Man*; Eleanor was canonised as "Everywoman" by Compton Mackenzie. Offspring of an urban mercantile dynasty, they mentally disowned the city: Theodore became the apologist for the frontier, Franklin and Eleanor the defenders of the small town. They share that regressiveness which is one of the oddest features of America – in a country of such imperial sway and extent, people are devoutly provincial in attitude; in a country of industrial might and jagged assertive skylines, everyone fears and detests cities and longs for the dreary greenery of a suburb or an exurb; in a country which is the centre of the world,

143

no-one seems to have heard of the rest of the world. An epic people hankers after a slumbrous pastoral fate: the American dream was rural, but the reality has turned out to be unacceptably urban. Theodore, born on East 20th Street in Manhattan, regarded cities as corruptingly slothful and debilitating because comfortable; for him the American epic consisted in exploration of the frontier. The prophecy has worked itself out to a bizarre conclusion. Once all frontiers were cleared, the Pacific coast represented an extreme limit and a curb to the expansive energies Theodore celebrated. Americans have responded by transforming California from a spatial frontier, which it can no longer be, into a temporal one – the twenty-first century is happening obscenely there, in a precarious futuristic pocket of time along a geological fault which will sooner or later tip it off into the sea. Already in Theodore's autobiography in 1913 he treats the wild West as obsolete for purposes of epic, gone with Atlantis to "the isle of ghosts and of strange dead memories", and he salutes its pastoral cultivation: "it was right and necessary that this life should pass, for the safety of our country lies in its being made the country of the small home-maker."

As the frontier retreated, rural homesteads were incorporated into small towns and suburbs, and it is this kind of community whose verities Eleanor guarded and extolled. In 1942 she contributed the text to a book of photographs by Frances Cooke Macgregor called *This Is America*, enlisting her image of the nation in the service of political propaganda. Her foreword describes the United States as a paradigm of the United Nations, "the example of what a family of nations can mean, since we in our nation are a family of varying races and religions", but the thinking is pastoral and domestic not imperial – having incorporated the world into itself, like Noah stocking the Ark with specimens of every living thing, America sees no further need to go out to meet the world; it is a global village, naturally isolationist. In opposition to the massed uniformity of European Fascism, Eleanor chooses to counterpoise not the continental grandeur of the United States but a single small town, Hingham in Massachusetts, and a single American family in which respect for personal freedoms creates a working model of democracy and convinces a refugee from Hitler that tyranny has no chance. Eleanor's microcosmic vision of America turns Hingham into a state farm, a mechanised toy-town of cheery conformity: the school playground also provides a laboratory experiment in democracy, where a bully may gain control temporarily but is soon "dealt with by the stern hand of majority rule".

Franklin D. Roosevelt (extreme left), Assistant Secretary to the Navy, launching the USS Tennessee, 1919.

Eleanor Roosevelt with their son Franklin Delano Jr., in 1909. The baby died in infancy. Far right: FDR on the family yacht, 1904.

146

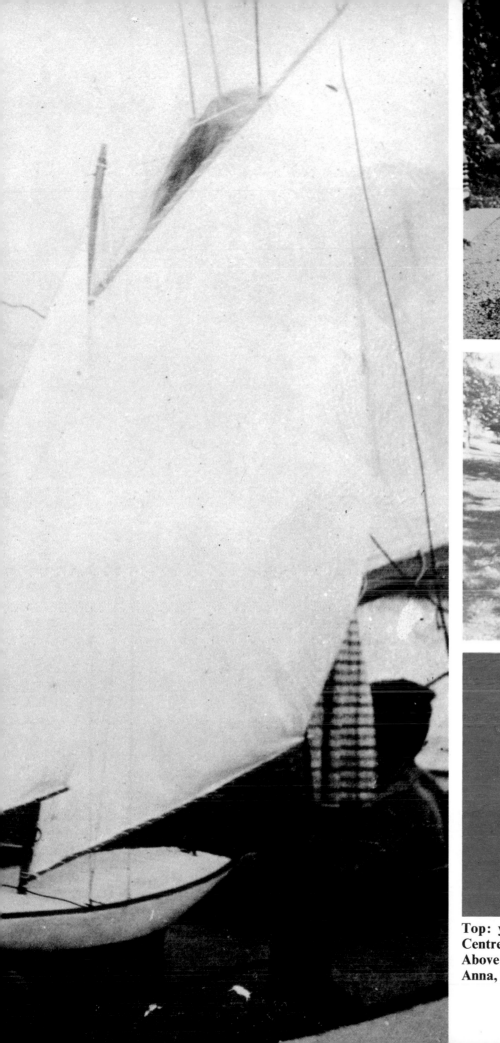

**Top: young FDR and his dog Budgy, 1884.
Centre: FDR and Eleanor on holiday, 1904.
Above: with their eldest children, James and
Anna, 1908. Left: FDR aboard his sloop, 1920.** 149

Sport, for Theodore a training in thrusting self-reliant character, has become in Eleanor's parable a discipline of adjustment to the communal team: treating English children evacuated from the bombings as unofficial ambassadors for the United Nations in Hingham, she warns them to work at mastering the game of baseball, "for the boy who didn't would have a lonely time here". Idealism requires her to see America through the wrong end of the telescope, to make a pastoral miniature of it – she gives away as much when, discussing the Italian population of Hingham, she argues that the small town is more a crucible of democracy than the city because "in the cities where there is a large representation from many foreign countries, the Italians, the Portuguese, the Germans, the Czechs, the Chinese have a tendency to form groups or 'colonies', and their foreign quality is accentuated. In the small town they are assimilated more quickly." In equalising, democracy must eliminate troublesome anti-social individualism; the city allows people to burrow into it in eccentric privacy, but the small town is intolerant of those who defy it, and has the means to censure them.

Theodore's was the America of Remington, whose drawings bragged of being "done in the open"; Franklin and Eleanor belonged in the more sedate, moralistic, indoor America Norman Rockwell invented for the covers of the *Saturday Evening Post*, and it is Rockwell who memorialised the America of the New Deal in the paintings he made in 1943 called *The Four Freedoms*. He remarked that "the job was too big for me. It should have been tackled by Michelangelo"; the epic theology of the Sistine Chapel has indeed descended from the ceiling and put on prosaic, truistic flesh in this series; the cellular scheme of universal history has been contracted, as in Eleanor's *This Is America*, into the exemplary activities of a small town; religious revelation has been translated into a political contract. Compton Mackenzie treats the New Deal neoclassically, as a modern Parthenon with Franklin a latter-day Pericles; Rockwell is the temple-builder, whose subjects are not the crises of myth but homely tales of domestic contentment. His freedoms are *Freedom of Speech* (a sturdy begrimed worker speaks up valiantly at a town meeting), *Freedom of Worship* (creased, weathered profiles bent in prayer), *Freedom from Want* (a swollen turkey is laid on a loaded table whose cloth gleams like an altar vestment, with a hungry family of acolytes lined up on either side), and *Freedom from Fear* (parents pensively tuck in their children, whose

High jinks at FDR's 52nd birthday party, 1934.
150 **Among the Roman 'maidens' is Eleanor (at rear, left).**

rag dolls litter the floor; the father holds a newspaper describing the blitz). The last is an image of Franklin's presidency – he soothed the millions who childishly depended on him by telling them they had nothing to fear but fear itself, just as Eleanor in her autobiography admits to having lied out of fear during her childhood, and persisted in the habit "until I reached the age when I realised that there was nothing to fear". What the touching rationalism of Franklin and Eleanor could not have anticipated was that, once Americans had been freed from fear, they would begin to fear their freedom. Liberalism has lost its nerve, and the conviction that the ills of society can be ministered to by goodwill alone now seems pitifully antediluvian. Eleanor's commentary in *This Is America* assumes that all problems can be disentangled by lucid exposition, that faults in reality are simple results of a learning deficiency, that the march of mind will triumph. She foresees the elimination of misery and want "as we gradually wipe out illiteracy, we improve our future government and build for a better nation".

Her death was the death of this liberal confidence: in the last decade Americans have been made to acknowledge the ineradicable sinfulness of human beings, the irreversibility of the damage already done to society and to a fouled, misused nature, and the impossibility of legislating evil out of the world. For every American, the disillusion is brutally personal. The country had promised him the privileges of Adam: liberated from history, the world all before him, he finds the paradise spoiled and wasted. His discovery of the grim inflexibility of the world outside him becomes a confession of his own fallibility. The abiding subject of American literature is the innocent's calamitous fall into experience: Europeans have an immemorial sense of evil from which they derive a suave talent for compromise, intrigue and discreet mendacity; every American must woundingly discover evil for himself, as if he had invented it. Eleanor the plain orphan immured in her grandmother's cheerless house on 37th Street or photographed on her wedding tour stiffly at ease in a gondola is an innocent from the novels of Henry James. Franklin the devious charmer belongs not in James's rigid moral universe but in the more specious, hedonistic world of Scott Fitzgerald: he had the princeliness of Gatsby, ruling, as John Gunther put it, "with a wand – even if it was an ivory cigarette holder", and the same beguiling emptiness, for like Gatsby he was a man who had turned self-protectively into an image. He once told Orson Welles, "you know, Orson, you 152 and I are the two best actors in America". Eleanor,

Franklin Roosevelt with a friend, Frances DeRham, recuperating in Florida after his polio attack.

however, possessed a rude integrity which sounds in her voice, whose high notes flapped out of control in plangent sincerity, in contrast with the insinuating, cozening delivery Franklin perfected in his radio addresses.

Eleanor wrote herself into a James novel in one piece of self-description: "I had painfully high ideals and a tremendous sense of duty, entirely unrelieved by any sense of humour or any appreciation of the weaknesses of human nature." The same sense of virtue as a righteous affliction and angelic amazement at corruption belongs to Millie Theale or Maggie Verver; but Eleanor managed to preserve a faith the heroines in the novels are compelled to sacrifice. Isabel Archer ends with the realisation that the world, after all, is very small; Eleanor's life ended, however, in gratified contemplation of its largeness. She was generalised into the itinerant conscience of humanity, and she universalised her domestic image of America, campaigning on behalf of a United Nations which she saw as a family of states joined for a sacramental Thanksgiving supper. Her career after the death of Franklin – as the American delegate to the first United Nations General Assembly, as a member of the Human Rights Commission, as an unquiet ghost taking guided tours of Hyde Park where she had assisted at the making of history, and as a sovereign influence inside the Democratic Party – is a remarkable case of the American promotion of a politician into a divinity. Purged of political function, Eleanor lived on under the blameless guard of a moral idea; released from the dutiful hospitality forced on her as Franklin's First Lady, she became, as Truman designated her, "First Lady of the World". The extension of her public life can be set revealingly against Jacqueline Kennedy's existence after her husband's death. She, like Eleanor, graduated from the confines of the White House to take over the world, first ruling as the tragic empress blotchily pictured on Andy Warhol's silk screens, then remarrying and removing herself into a Harold Robbins fantasy of conspicuous, orgiastic consumption. Eleanor trudged around the world in the fatiguing pursuit of an idea; Mrs Onassis shuttles from one continent to another in the listless pursuit of distraction. Eleanor made a gift of herself to humanity. Reminding herself of her age, she said, "Think! I am over sixty, which means that I only have 15 years left for useful public service!", and she even considered her autobiography not as a monument to herself but as a possible tool

154 **The 'Little White House', Warm Springs, Georgia, where FDR died, 1945. Right: a cover for _Vanity Fair_, 1934.**

The Presidential campaign, 1932. Top: Governor Roosevelt at home in the Executive Mansion, Albany, New York, in July as the campaign began. Centre: a triumphal ride through the streets of Seattle, Washington. Above: canvassing votes from his car in West Virginia. Left: a packed Hollywood Bowl to hear Roosevelt speak. In the election he beat the incumbent President Hoover by a huge margin. 157

HOLLYWOOD

★ ★

Pat O'Brien   Rosalind Russell   Doug
Alice Faye   James Cagney   Dorothy L
Edward G. Robinson   Andy Devine
Robert Benchley   Sally Eilers   H
Ritz Brothers   Virgina Bruce   Joan

AND HUN

3¢ DAILY TIMES CHICAGO'S PICTURE NEWSPAPER

LATE NEWS PICTURES

440,028
95% IN CHICAGO AND SUBURBS

WEDNESDAY, NOVEMBER 8, 1944   60 Pages

THAT MAN'S HERE AGAIN!

Latest returns

	Popular vote	Electoral vote		Projected vote		Popular vote
F. D. R.	18,500,456	426	Green	1,945,856	Lucas	1,741,019

For ROOSEVELT ★ ★

Fairbanks Jr.   Melvyn Douglas   Sylvia Sydney
George Raft   Miriam Hopkins   Hugh Herbert
Mitchell   Betty Grable   Henry Fonda
Bogart   Claude Rains
James Gleason   Jane Wyman
EDS OF OTHERS

Outdoor Advertising Co.

Above: wide backing from the stars, as Hollywood names throw their support behind FDR for a third term as President in 1940. Far left: the President (and his cigarette holder) in jaunty mood. Centre: the unprecedented fourth term – a big wartime victory for FDR in 1944. Near left: Louis Howe, loyal adviser and speech-writer to Eleanor and FDR from the first Senate campaign in 1912, at his home in Westport, Massachusetts. Right: triumph for the New Deal – in the mid-term elections during FDR's first presidency, the Democrats sweep the board.

Peacetime ally: FDR with Churchill at the Atlantic Charter Conference, August 1941, before the U.S. entered the war.

for the use of others: "there is nothing particularly interesting to one's life story unless people can say as they read it, 'Why this is like what I have been through. Perhaps, after all, there is a way to work it out'." Mrs Onassis has likewise willed herself to the world, but as a spectacular diversion rather than as a moral counsel.

As Eleanor has become a grandmotherly angel folding her wings over the world, her beatitude intensified as old age ripened her youthful gawky plainness into a splendid genial ugliness, so Franklin has been treated as a divinity by H. G. Wells – but a god of brooding omniscient thought not, like Eleanor, of affectionate evangelistic concern. Cartoonists indeed presented Franklin as a figure adept in magic, re-animating decrepit myths: *Punch* in 1932 drew him as Ganymede, cup-bearer to the gods, borne uncomfortably aloft into a blazing sky by a rather *louche* eagle with an Uncle Sam hat and a cigar clamped in

its beak; Franklin himself stretches his hat out in the air, as if busking for donations. Halfway between eulogy and lampoon, the cartoon seems uncertain about how far to trust Franklin's heroism or how far to mock it. Elsewhere, cartoonists freed him from his wheel-chair and made him a brawny hunter like Theodore, casting him as Orpheus taming savage beasts through the soothing influence of common sense or as a lion tamer brandishing a whip at the bestial financial crisis and promising it, "you're going out like a lamb!" The cartoons granted Franklin a dubious heroism; but Wells, visiting the United States as a 'social biologist' in 1934–5, simply promoted him to a god, whose rule was a benign superintendence of thought. Wells interpreted the office of the presidency as a near-religious one, except that the president was not the bearded curmudgeon of the old faiths, not a gruff dogmatist, but a purely contemplative divinity whose role was "to sublimate,

Wartime victor: an ailing Roosevelt between Churchill and Joseph Stalin at the Yalta Conference, February 1945.

clarify and express the advancing thought of the community"; like one of Shaw's Ancients in *Back to Methuselah* he belonged to a future state of metabiology in which problems would be solved as soon as they were understood. Franklin becomes in Wells's description a fine nerve-centre, a mental mechanism, "a ganglion for reception, expression, transmission, combination, and realisation", symbolically surrounded by a group of advisers known as the Brains Trust. Hitler decried this group as a conspiratorial coven of parasitic Jews, but for Wells they signified the submission of politics to intellect.

In truth Franklin was not a sovereign intelligence, nor was Eleanor a sovereign conscience. One of his aides gave the lie to Wells's notion when, having been asked what Franklin thought about a specific issue, he replied, "Oh, the President never thinks." Instead, Franklin guessed, vacillating precariously between the State's monopolistic right to adjust production

and restrict trade and quite different policies devoted to social reform, relying on gamesmanship, the exhilaration of risk and the cajoling distribution of favours to win over Congress and the electorate. In the same way Eleanor did not wait on moral victories, but worked cannily and obstinately in her own defence and against her opponents. Her innocence was not fragile and ingenuous, like Millie Theale's, but barbed and guileful, like Maggie Verver's. Although she disclaimed any interest in power – modestly attributing the cheers of the Democratic Convention in Chicago in 1952 to reverence for her husband's memory, protesting always with infuriating coyness that she was a simple woman who knew nothing of politics – she was often able, with pleasing symmetry, to serve the right while paying back a political enemy. An example is her campaign to expel Carmine de Sapio from Tammany Hall. His boss rule was an offence against democracy; but his more pertinent crime was 161

Above: American poverty – the target of the New Deal. Right: FDR signing the Declaration of War against Japan.

to have engineered a political defeat for her son Franklin. During the 1956 presidential election she was demurely venomous at the expense of both Eisenhower and Nixon. Her technique was to establish her elderly benevolence with an initial compliment, and then to strike out with an air of regretting the truths she was obliged to tell. When an interviewer asked her if she thought Eisenhower too much inclined towards big business at the expense of "the little guy", she began with an indignant denial: "Oh, no! The President is a good man and he would want always to do the right thing as he saw it, but he has a great admiration for the achievement of the successful business man because he has never been a successful business man and you always admire what you really don't understand." The remark combines snobbery – the Roosevelts were successful business men – with a neat slur by association. In the case of Nixon, she first apologised for disliking him, then allowed that he might have matured, then finally mentioned the case of Helen Gahagan Douglas as proof that his was a character unfit for public life. She was equally unscrupulous in her support of Adlai Stevenson, accusing his rival Kennedy of pusillanimity during the McCarthy years and directing sly innuendos against Joseph Kennedy's vow "to spend any money to make his son the first Catholic president

of this country".

Ultimately, however, nothing one can find out about Theodore's infantile insensitivity or Franklin's reliance on bluff to avert national catastrophe or Eleanor's crafty vindictiveness is of much importance, because American politics is less of a struggle for power than a shadow-play of images, and every participant becomes an actor, consciously fictionalising himself, as Franklin's remark to Orson Welles reveals. If it is impossible or improper to be real, you might just as well be beguilingly unreal. The recent tragedies of Johnson and Nixon consisted in not finding masks to fit. Nixon's peculiar error was to maintain a private life which was not available to the public, to closet himself in shameful secrecy listening onanistically to tape recordings of his own voice. The Roosevelts made themselves public possessions, and the truth about them must be sought in the official images, not in private disclosures of frailty. They remain sacrosanct – strenuous wood-chopping canal-building Theodore; infirm Franklin learning compassion during his years of paralytic retirement and emerging from rural privacy for his rendezvous with destiny; fubsy Eleanor the sleeping beauty, as Archibald MacLeish called her, waiting among "the thorns and thickets of the decaying castle of the dying age into which she was born" to be recalled to life.

162

The Roosevelts and their thirteen grandchildren assembled for FDR's fourth inauguration in 1945.

When Franklin Roosevelt died on April 12 1945, he had been President for over 12 years. The shock to America was enormous, exemplified by the face of the Negro serviceman watching the coffin begin its journey from Warm Springs to the grave (above) in Hyde Park, New York.

ROCKEFELLER

Edward Jay Epstein

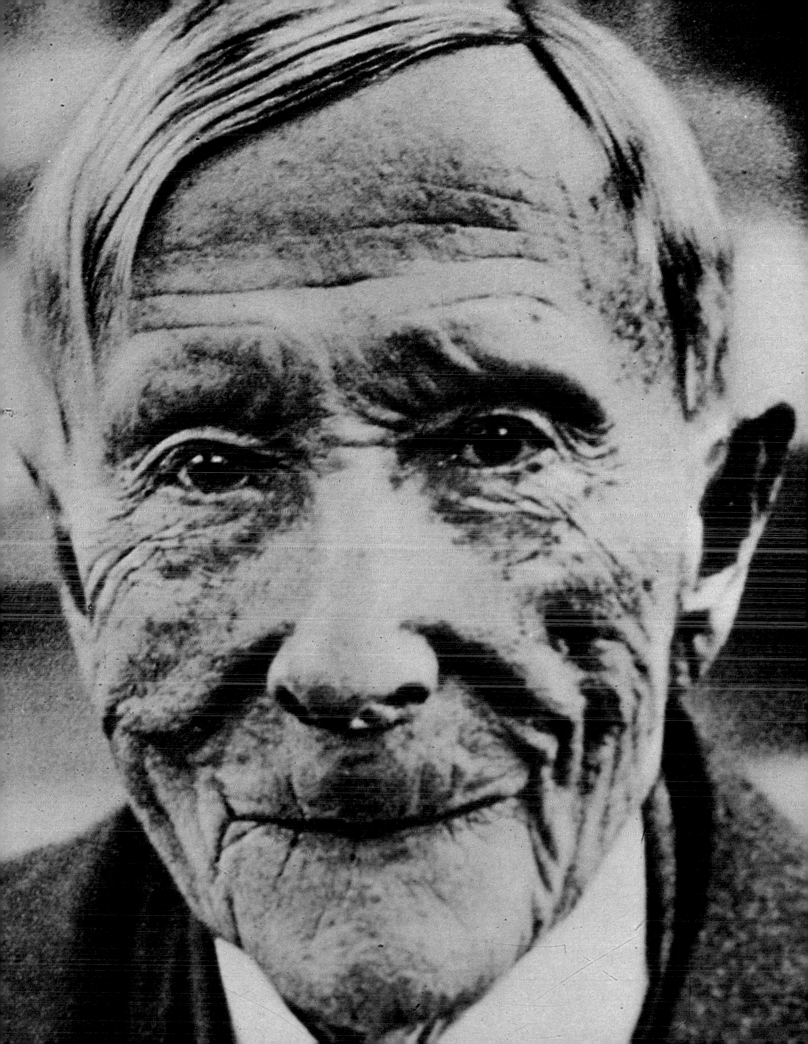

Surrounded by round-the-clock armed guards and a barricade of barbed wire, the body of Laura Celeste Spelman Rockefeller awaited burial for some twenty weeks between March and August, 1915, while her husband John Davidson Rockefeller avoided angry mobs and process servers. At that time Rockefeller was perhaps the wealthiest man the modern world had ever known. His personal fortune was equal to 2 per cent. of the total gross national product of the United States and this did not include the vast fortune passed on to the rest of his family which then controlled banks, railways and newly-created philanthropic foundations. The Standard Oil Companies which he had created and in which he still held a major (25 per cent.) interest, then refined more than 90 per cent. of the oil sold in America and most of that of the rest of the world. Its political power was such that it was accused of doing everything with state legislatures except 'refining them'.

Yet despite such economic resources, Rockefeller had become an object of hatred and derision in America; he could not bury his wife of more than half a century for fear that the body might be desecrated or that he might be subpoenaed at the funeral by any of a dozen governmental bodies investigating his activities. Indeed, for more than a decade Rockefeller had been hounded by relentless muckrakers, who portrayed him as a ruthless robber baron; investigated continually by state attorney generals and congressional committees who turned him into a fugitive from his own family; and denounced by political leaders of both parties as an 'arch-criminal'. Even charities hesitated to accept Rockefeller's 'tainted money' on the ground, as Senator Robert M. Lafollette argued, that "he gives with two hands but robs with many . . . he is the greatest criminal of the age".

In 1915 public passions were further aroused against Rockefeller by widely-circulated reports of massacres of women and children at the Colorado Fuel and Iron company which his family controlled. In such an atmosphere wealth was of little use in quieting public opinion. Effective power, Rockefeller learned, depended on control of not merely pipelines, refineries, railways and banks, but also of the leaders and conduits of public opinion. And just as the old Rockefeller was able to organise industries systematically for great profit, his heirs learned to organise just as efficiently the perceptions and passions that constitute that vague realm known as 'public opinion'. As Nelson Aldrich Rockefeller testified 60 years later when he was being considered for vice president of the United States, "power *per se* is good or bad depending on how it is used [but] power is essential".

171

The benefactor – John D. Rockefeller as he liked to see himself, Christmas 1925.

John D. with his only son John D. Jr. (standing), his daughter-in-law, and his six grandchildren.

John D. Rockefeller, born on a farm in New York State in 1839, was the son of an adventurer who had made a small fortune selling patent medicines and cancer cures which owed their success, if they were like other 'botanic medicines' of their day, to an opium base. When John D. reached the age of 20, his father advanced him sufficient funds to buy a half interest in a commodity commission business in Cleveland. That same year, 1859, the first oil well in America was drilled at Titusville, Pennsylvania, and part of the oil was shipped down the Cuyohoga River to Cleveland for refining and then re-shipping to New York. In the next few years, the oil fields of Pennsylvania became the main source of kerosene for the entire world and young Rockefeller moved his commodity business from grain, hay and meat into oil. By the time he was 26 he had bought out his partners in what was then the largest refinery in Cleveland, and formed what was eventually known as the Standard Oil Company. Rockefeller immediately foresaw that transportation, not production of oil or retail sales, would be the key to controlling the burgeoning industry. Any refiner who could ship the oil for a few cents a barrel less than other refiners to the major

market in New York would drive his competitors out of business. With this insight, Rockefeller proceeded to dominate the oil industry.

By negotiating a 'rebate' on each barrel of oil his refinery shipped, Rockefeller received a secret rate which allowed him to undersell his competitors in New York. Since greater profits for all proceeded from the lower shipping rate, it was in the self-interest of competing refineries to join Standard, and most of them rushed to exchange their stock for either Standard stock or cash. By 1882 the Standard Oil Company, reorganised by Rockefeller's lawyers into a 'trust' (which had previously had a benign meaning), controlled 95 per cent. of the refining capacity in the United States. And Rockefeller, at the age of 43, controlled Standard Oil which now expanded into all phases of the oil industry – exploration, production, shipping and marketing.

Before Americans were subject to income tax the dividends from Standard Oil made Rockefeller by far the wealthiest man in the country. Eventually the government – first the states and then the federal – moved against Standard Oil and laws were passed against 'rebates' and 'trusts'. Finally, in 1911, under

Tycoon at Christmas, c. 1930. John D. Rockefeller did, in fact, give away more than 530 million dollars.

the crusading zeal of President Theodore Roosevelt, the Standard Oil trust was dissolved into 33 separate companies of which the Rockefellers remained large shareholders (receiving about 25 per cent. of the shares of each new company).

Rockefeller's organisational genius was not limited to oil. During the boom of the 1890s, he bought up a large share of the entire Pacific North-west, including railways, steel mills, paper mills, factories, ore deposits, lumber, and vast tracts of real estate, including the entire city of Everett in the state of Washington. A dedicated Baptist, he founded the University of Chicago on the condition that it be "aggressively Christian" with no "infidel teachers". He also pioneered the creation of tax-exempt foundations for the "well being of mankind" (just before income tax laws were passed in the United States) which changed the shape of 'philanthropy' in the United States, and insulated a large portion of his fortune from modern taxation.

Since Rockefeller lived to the amazing age of 98, his only child John Jr did not inherit full control over the fortune – and foundations – until he was 63 and nearly retired. When 'Junior', as he was called,

attempted to take an active part in the family business in the first decade of the twentieth century, he found that he was being held personally responsible for the reign of terror and bloodshed in industrial America, which reached its height in 1915 after the Rockefeller-controlled Colorado Fuel and Iron company was closed down by workers who demanded the right to collective bargaining and the enforcement of state labour laws which the company had been ignoring for years. The company, with the Rockefellers' active support, called in a private army of gunmen and the state militia to crush the strike and in the ensuing violence the tent camp of miners at Ludlow, Colorado, was ruthlessly sprayed with machine gun fire and burned to the ground. Along with several workers, 11 children and two women were killed in what became known nationally as the 'Ludlow Massacre'. With great gusto the national Press used the image of 'roasted children' to portray 'Junior' as a new national villain. Years later Junior told his official biographer Raymond B. Fosdick, that the Colorado strike was "one of the most important things that ever happened to the family" – if nothing else, it demonstrated to him that the future of the

173

Ludlow miners' camp, Colorado, in ruins after soldiers had fired on striking workers, 1915.

family depended on creating a new public image, one outside corporate business. An entire new public relations industry was created to focus public attention completely on the charitable work of the family. Junior turned the family business over to professional managers, and undertook such projects as saving the redwood trees in California and creating three new national parks. He financed crusades such as the Interchurch World Movement, an unsuccessful inter-denominationalist effort "to Christianise the world". He also financed the effort to prohibit the consumption of alcohol in the United States.

He assiduously avoided politics, though he married Abby Aldrich, daughter of Senator Winthrop Aldrich, the most important Republican leader of his time. His only important business venture, according to his biographer, was the erection of Rockefeller Center, a colossal office building complex on Fifth Avenue in the heart of New York City which he bravely built at the height of the depression in the 1930s. Rockefeller Center, which today provides some 10 million square feet of office space and brings in rent in the order of a hundred million dollars a

year for the Rockefeller family, instantly became a major tourist attraction with its Art Deco murals of workers in factories and Radio City from which NBC broadcasts its programmes. The Center also provided 'Room 5600' which consists in fact of the entire 55th and 56th floors of the tallest building, from where the family's far-flung finances and public relations are professionally managed.

The public relations operation in Room 5600 became especially effective. To this day information about the Rockefellers is stored in either 'sensitive' or 'public' files. The former, which might conflict with the image being promoted, is embargoed or destroyed, while the latter is disseminated to writers of authorised biographies and journalists. Through the careful cultivation of the Press, the public image of public enemy that Rockefeller Junior inherited was subtly transformed to one of a public benefactor. When he died at the age of 86, his six children had already ascended to the highest strata of the social and political order. No longer outcasts, the Rockefeller heirs had become the American aristocracy.

* * * * *

The John D. Rockefellers, Senior and Junior: Junior was 63 before his father died in 1937.

The Rockefeller heirs grew up in the family enclave at Pocantico Hills, a private fiefdom of some 3500 acres on the Hudson River 50 miles north of New York City, which at times employed as many as 1500 servants, bodyguards, secretaries and other retainers to care for the eleven baronial mansions on the estate. The play house where the heirs spent much of their childhood had an indoor swimming pool, indoor tennis and squash courts, billiard tables, two bowling alleys and closets full of toys. There were also such recreational facilities on the estate as a private golf course, stables, 80 miles of private riding trails and six swimming pools. The eldest heir and only daughter, Abby, was born in 1903. Like other women in the Rockefeller family, she was carefully shielded from any public role by the Rockefeller managers who invested her trust funds and arranged her political contributions. Married three times she was rarely mentioned in the Press or even the authorised biographies of the family.

The eldest son, John Davidson Rockefeller III, was born in 1906 at a time when his illustrious grandfather was still hiding out from government investigators. Able to recall the public outcry over the Ludlow Massacre, 'Mr John', as he was called, chose like his father to establish himself in philanthropies rather than business. He travelled to Japan immediately after graduating from Princeton in 1929 – the first of sixteen such trips – and thereafter concentrated his efforts on assisting Asian nations to control their populations. Serving in the military government that occupied Japan after the Second World War and then as a consultant to the U.S. Peace Settlement Mission in Japan, he poured considerable money into developing the entente between Japan and the United States.

Rockefeller Junior's second son, Nelson, born in 1908 was by far the most publicly ambitious of the heirs. His first major sphere of activity was political propaganda. Before he was 30 he became a director of the Creole Petroleum Company, the subsidiary of Standard Oil of New Jersey which then provided it with most of its foreign oil from the enormous reserves it controlled in Venezuela. In examining the position of Creole Oil in Venezuela Nelson became convinced that public relations in the host country was essential for retaining control over Latin American oil. In 1939 he and his associates from the Chase

176 **Family homes: J.D.'s birthplace and (top) Golf House.**

Manhattan Bank and Rockefeller Center prepared a three-page memorandum for President Franklin D. Roosevelt which suggested the creation of a government agency to counter Nazi propaganda and covert infiltration in Latin America. FDR, on the recommendation of an adviser (who later received a loan from Nelson Rockefeller), named Nelson in 1940 to head the new agency which became known as the Co-ordinator of Inter-American Affairs (CIAA), or simply as the Rockefeller Office. Before America entered the War, according to a former staff member of the Rockefeller Office, "almost all our efforts were directed into organising the pro-Western élites of Venezuela and Brazil into a private network of

influence". Almost exclusively, Latin American business executives and public opinion leaders were recruited into this network. Then, after the United States entered the War, the Rockefeller Office directed its major efforts towards outright propaganda.

To gain control over the media of Latin America during the War, Rockefeller obtained a ruling from the U.S. Treasury Department which exempted the cost of advertisements placed by American corporations that were cooperating with the Rockefeller Office from taxation. This tax-exempt advertising eventually constituted more than 40 per cent. of all radio and newspaper revenues in Latin America. By selectively directing this advertising towards newspapers and radio stations that accepted guidance from his office – and simultaneously denying it to media which he deemed uncooperative or pro-Nazi – he skilfully managed to gain economic leverage over the major sources of news throughout South America. Moreover, as the newsprint shortage became critical in South America, his office made sure that the indispensable newsprint licences were allocated only to friendly newspapers. With a staff of some 1,200 in the United States, including mobilised journalists, advertising experts and public opinion analysts, and some $140 million in government funds (expended over five years), the Rockefeller Office mounted a propaganda effort virtually unprecedented in the annals of 177

American history. It was also formative education for young Rockefeller in the vulnerabilities of the Press.

From the beginning it became apparent that news was not the product of journalistic investigation, but of special interest groups. If economic pressure could be brought against the owners, and incentives given to editors, news in Latin America could be surreptitiously authored in Washington rather than Berlin or elsewhere. To this end, the Rockefeller Office provided not only 'canned' editorials, photographs, exclusives, feature stories and other such news material, but manufactured its own mass circulation magazines, supplements, pamphlets and newsreels. To ensure understanding of the 'issues' being advanced in Latin America, the Office sent 13,000 carefully selected 'opinion leaders', a weekly newsletter which was to help them 'clarify' the issues of the day. The CIAA also arranged trips to the United States for the most influential editors in Latin America (and later scholarships for their children). More than 1200 newspapers and 200 radio stations, which survived the economic warfare, were fed a daily diet of some 30,000 words of 'news' in Spanish and Portuguese, which were disseminated by cooperating news agencies and radio networks in the United States to their clients in Latin America. By the end of the War, the CIAA estimated that more than 75 per cent. of the news of the world that reached Latin America originated from Washington where it was tightly controlled and monitored by the Rockefeller Office and State Department. The operation, Rockefeller realised, required only sufficient money and talent.

After the War Nelson divided his time between managing various Rockefeller interests and in serving in various government administrations in Washington. He served Truman as chairman of the International Development Advisory Board and later Eisenhower as an under-secretary of the Department of Housing, Education and Welfare and as a special assistant to the president for foreign affairs.

The middle heir, Laurance Spelman Rockefeller, was born in New York City in 1910 and, like all his

178   **Winthrop Rockefeller, a war hero in the Pacific, with an admirer at the Stork Club, 1942.**

brothers, attended an Ivy League college, Princeton. (The lone sister Abby was sent to finishing school.) While his elder brothers pursued careers in philanthropy and politics, Laurance became an entrepreneur. Before the War he provided the financing for Captain Eddie Rickenbacker, the First World War aviation ace, to buy the aviation division from General Motors and turn it into Eastern Airlines, which subsequently became profitable (after it was awarded the highly lucrative route to Puerto Rico by the government). Laurance was also instrumental in financing the McDonnell Aircraft Corporation which became a prime supplier of aircraft for the United States Navy during the Second World War and later developed the world-famous Phantom fighter. Laurance spent his war as a lieutenant-commander in the production division of the Navy, superintending for the most part the relation between the Navy and aviation contractors such as McDonnell Aircraft. Realising that the government would soon be employing missiles to replace bombers he found a New Jersey company, Reaction Motors, Inc., which had developed an early rocket engine along the lines of the captured German V-2 rocket. When the United States government bought the Reaction Motors engine for its newly-developed Viking missile, Rockefeller made another small fortune. As missiles became more sophisticated, he invested heavily in Marquadt Aviation whose stock value increased 1000 per cent after it became publicly known that the government was buying its ram jet rocket engine for its next generation of missiles. During the 1950s, Laurance continued to invest heavily in newly-formed companies specialising in military technology, and the profits generated by the fluctuation of the stock prices of these companies proved a useful source of funds for his politically ambitious elder brother, Nelson.

Rockefeller's fourth son, Winthrop, born in 1912, proved to be somewhat of a black sheep. Unlike his brothers, who earned honours degrees at college, Winthrop dropped out of Yale and worked as a roustabout in the Texas oil fields of a subsidiary of Standard Oil of New Jersey – at a time when the Rockefeller family was desperately attempting to dissociate its public image from that of the oil companies which provided its original wealth. When he refused to leave the oil business, he was appointed a junior executive at Socony-Vacuum Oil (of which the Rockefeller family owned the largest single share). While his brothers tended the administrative side of the War, Winthrop sought out a combat assignment in the Pacific and after being wounded, emerged as a decorated war hero. In 1953 he left the eastern base of the family and moved to Arkansas, buying a sizeable portion of the state. He developed a 50,000-acre cattle ranch there which he also used for intellectual seminars and research. He also established a strong political base in Arkansas, and eventually the southern wing of the Republican party.

Rockefeller Junior's youngest child, David, was the only heir born after the Ludlow Massacre, in 1915. After graduating from Harvard and attending the London School of Economics he received his Doctor of Philosophy degree in 1940 from the University of Chicago – and then became a trustee of the institution his grandfather founded. After serving briefly as an unpaid intern to the Mayor of New York City, and then as a Housing Administrator for the Office of Defence, he joined the Army in 1942 where he rapidly rose as an intelligence officer to the rank of Assistant Military Attaché in the American Embassy in Paris. He was admitted to the French Legion of Honour in 1945. His real ambition in life was international banking. Immediately after the War, David went to work for the Chase National Bank, of which his uncle, Winthrop W. Aldrich, was then Chairman of the Board. As an assistant manager of the foreign department, David specialised in opening branches and expanding the bank's influence in the areas of Latin America in which his elder brother had established interests. The former co-ordinator, Nelson, had quietly transferred the operation of the wartime Rockefeller Office to two Rockefeller-owned entities – IBEC (International Basic Economics Corporation), a profit-making corporation which was investing in agriculture and marketing companies in South America – and taking full advantage of the network of businessmen which Rockefeller had assembled during the War – and AIA, the American International Association for Economic and Social Development which encompassed non-profit activities such as grants and scholarships, thus maintaining liaisons between local government officials and leading members of the Latin American Press. Laurance, through his airline and hotel operations, had by this time become deeply involved in business in Puerto Rico, where David conveniently opened a Chase branch. The young banker was also successful in establishing a close working relation in Panama with the closely-knit financial and political families that more or less ran the government of that country.

With Rockefeller interests owning the largest block of stock in Chase, and two seats on its Board of Directors, David rapidly ascended to the presidency of the bank in 1961, when he was only 44. The Chase Manhattan Bank – as it was called after it absorbed the Manhattan Bank in 1955 – was even then one of the three most powerful banks in the United States with assets over $10 billion. As head of this international financial institution, David criss-crossed the world numerous times during the Sixties, dining with kings and heads of states, and compiling index cards of some 20,000 acquaintances on whom he could possibly call for assistance. A member of the élite Council on Foreign Relations since 1942 and an active participant in the public and private gatherings of the so-called Eastern Establishment, David became the single most effective spokesman for the entire American business community.

* * * * *

By the late 1950s the brothers Rockefeller had firmly laid the surface as well as the underground foundation for political power in America. Their public image had been elevated from that of outcasts to that of dedicated public servants through a 40-year long refinement of public data about the family. Through their tax exempt foundations and philanthropies, and the dispensation of over a billion dollars to intellectual and scientific enterprises, the brothers had also woven a strong, if sometimes invisible, web of influence that touched in one way or another virtually all the activities of those who articulate and advocate issues in the mainstream of public life.

180 **John D. Rockefeller Jr. poses with a Negro girl.**

In 1956, demonstrating the scope of their influence, the brothers involved more than a hundred of the most influential men in America in a four-year-long dialogue on various issues of concern to the family. The agenda for these panels was planned by Henry A. Kissinger who, before he became Presidents' Nixon and Ford's national security adviser and Secretary of State, had been on retainer for Nelson Rockefeller for a dozen years, and Francis A. Jamaison the brilliant public relations specialist for Nelson Rockefeller. The Rockefeller panels were aimed at forming a consensus among the decision-making elite on such issues of the time as 'foreign policy', 'the communist threat,' responses to 'concealed aggression', 'nuclear strategy', 'economic policies', and the 'reconstruction of the democratic consensus'. By 1958 when the centrist position on all these issues was sufficiently clarified, Nelson Rockefeller, the most political and out-going of the brothers, declared his intention of seeking the Republican nomination for governor of New York State in the approaching November elections.

Since no Rockefeller had sought elective office before, the family organisation had to marshal special resources to ensure that Nelson received the nomination of the Republican party. At the time the Republican party in New York State was controlled by a few dozen county leaders in upstate cities, such as Elmira, Syracuse, Rochester and Albany. In New York City, the one place where the Rockefellers could most easily bring their financial and foundation power to bear on politicians, the Republican organisation was moribund if not totally deceased.

To be sure, the most influential upstate Republicans were independent businessmen and responsive to a limited degree to pressure from banks lending them money. Both the Chase Manhattan Bank (which the family through David controlled) and the National City Bank (of which his cousin was Chairman of the Board) could thus exert some pressure on Nelson's behalf. But the heavy hand of New York's banks also created strong antipathy to Rockefeller from the more independent-minded county leaders and it rapidly became clear to Nelson that he would need some more discreet connection with these men. To this end Nelson made arrangements with two professional political operators in New York State – Malcolm Wilson, a legislator who could deal expediently with the Westchester County Republicans, and Lyman Judson Morhouse, the state Republican Chairman, who was also, according to his defence at a subsequent bribery trial, a professed 'influence' seller in New York State. For his part, Morhouse immediately selected Nelson

John D. as he liked others to see him – the rich man and his burden of responsibility.

Rockefeller as the chairman of the Committee on the Preparation of a State Constitutional Convention, which provided convenient access to all grass-root Republican leaders in the state. But behind the scenes, Morhouse played an even more important role in helping Rockefeller make his separate peace with various county leaders, by collecting cash contributions of one sort or another from pro-Rockefeller sources and redistributing them where necessary to help towards securing the Republican nomination for Rockefeller. Rockefeller not only succeeded in easily winning the election, but provided more than half the campaign funds for the entire Republican party.

As both chairman of the party and the director of the powerful State Thruway Commission (to which Rockefeller, by prior arrangement, appointed him), Morhouse continued his service as a political bagman and all-purpose fixer during the first three years of the Rockefeller administration. During these years he collected hundreds of thousands of dollars from watch manufacturers, drug laboratories, lessees for space at the airport, highway contractors (through the Good Road Association), radio and television licensees in New York State, detective agencies seeking conces-

sions at the World's Fair, large corporations such as Lucius D. Clay's Continental Can, and others seeking indulgences from the State of New York. Whether Morhouse was collecting this money for his own account, or simply 'laundering' the money for undercover politics (disguising its original source), Rockefeller could not have been totally unaware of the magnitude of the operation. For example, in June 1959, Rockefeller witnessed Morhouse receive a hundred thousand dollars in a 'shoebox' at a Republican Party dinner, and ordered the money returned because, he later testified, he "was fearful that this was race track money [from] people who wanted to get a licence for a racetrack".

While such backstage redistributions of cash from those seeking and owed favours was hardly novel in New York State politics, Rockefeller was able to change the rules of the game by infusing vast amounts of money into the subterranean system through ingenious use of his own personal fortune and the institutions under his family's sway. Providing Morhouse with cash, untraceable in any way to the Rockefellers, required, however, the unique institutional resources of the Rockefeller Brothers and Associates 181 in Room 5600 of Rockefeller Center. Thus Laurance Rockefeller, at Nelson's specific request, nominally sold Morhouse 2500 shares in a privately held corporation, the Marks Oxygen Company, which supplied liquid fuel for the expanding missile programme, for $25,000. No money actually changed hands, since Laurance loaned Morhouse the funds for buying the stock. Eighteen months later, after much financial manoeuvring, Laurance bought the stock back from Morhouse for $79,375, leaving a profit of more than $50,000 in Morhouse's account. After the profit for Morhouse, part of the proceeds from the Oxygen Company was used to reimburse the Rockefellers for 4000 shares of Geophysics Corporation of America deposited in Morhouse's account which rose almost tenfold from $6 to $56 a share, and left Morhouse with a paper profit of a quarter of a million dollars which could have been used at his discretion.

Mr Morhouse, unfortunately, was never able to use the money for political purposes, since he was inadvertently overheard on a wire tap arranging a hundred thousand dollar bribe for obtaining a liquor licence for the Playboy Club in New York, and had to sell a portion of his stock to defray legal expenses. When he was convicted of conspiracy and bribery, Rockefeller, as governor, pardoned him on medical grounds before he could spend time in prison.

As governor, Rockefeller demonstrated that he was a masterful orchestrator of both the levers and symbols of political power. He immediately found that the condition that satisfied most of the politically important interest groups in the state was the massive government construction programme. Journalistic critics of Rockefeller in those years who attributed his monumental building projects to some sort of psychological 'erection complex' underestimated the political profit such vast expenditures on construction gained for him from key unions and business interests in the state. The political problem, which restrained Rockefeller's predecessors from constructing public works on a scale of the Egyptian pyramids, was that they could not be paid for out of taxes, since the wrath of the electorate over tax increases would far outweigh any advantages from special interest groups pleased with the expenditures. Nor was it easy to finance these projects through issuing long-term bonds, which had the obvious advantage of deferring tax burdens to future generations of taxpayers, because such bonds had to be approved by the electorate at a referendum, according to the state's constitution.

With characteristic ingenuity, Nelson Rockefeller over-rode this stumbling block to expansion by devising with the connivance of John N. Mitchell (who subsequently became Nixon's Attorney General) special authorities which could issue virtually unlimited amounts of long-term debt without the approval of the voters. Of course, the bonds issued by these authorities were not legally backed by the full faith of the state, since they by-passed the constitutional requirement of a referendum. Rockefeller pledged the full moral authority of the state behind the bonds, and Mitchell, then a leading bond lawyer in New York City, rendered an opinion that this was tantamount to a state obligation. 'Moral obligation' bonds, as they came to be called, proved a bonanza for the large banks, especially the Chase Manhattan Bank, which sold them to institutions and the public. In all, Rockefeller raised over $6 billion through pledging this 'moral obligation' to substitute for the more conventional type of state bond.

Under anyone but Rockefeller, there might have been great resistance among state officials to issuing such unorthodox bonds, especially since they entailed no legal commitment to the financial community. Rockefeller, however, succeeded in engendering an unusual degree of loyalty among his key officials by quietly distributing to them more than one and a half million dollars in cash from his private fortune. Typically, Rockefeller's secret gifts (or loans which became gifts) went to such instrumental state officials as the Superintendent of Banks, members of the State Housing Financing agency, the commissioner of the Department of Environmental Conservation (which oversaw a two billion dollar pure water construction programme), the commissioner of Housing and Community Renewal, the president of the Urban Development Corporation (which built billions of dollars' worth of housing and industrial parks), the commissioner of Taxation and Finance, the chairman of the Metropolitan Transportation Authority, the Director of Communications, and his staff assistants. Not only did some officials receive hundreds of thousands of dollars from Rockefeller, but they also received future employment sponsored by his family foundations and the very profitable management of their investments in newly formed defence contractors and other corporations selected by the family advisers in Room 5600 in Rockefeller Center. While Rockefeller's ability to distribute largesse when necessary may have helped cement the loyalty of the officials necessary to the success of his unconventional devices for financing construction projects, it appeared to conflict with Article 200 of the New York State Penal Code which explicitly prohibits conferring "any benefit upon a public servant for having engaged in official conduct . . ."

Rockefeller, who conferred millions of dollars of such benefits on public officials, simply asserted, when the gifts were finally made public by an FBI investigation in 1974, that he gave the cash to the public servants out of his esteem for them, not out of any motive related to the work they were performing for him as governor – and because of his carefully managed reputation as a philanthropist the matter was not referred to a court for adjudication. Eventually, after Rockefeller left office in 1973, the State of New York refused to assist the first of these authorities, the Urban Development Corporation, by then a $2 billion entity, threatened with bankruptcy, since it was not in fact legally bound by Rockefeller's pledge of a 'moral obligation'. When the Urban Development Corporation subsequently defaulted and left its bond holders stranded, the value of all such moral obligation bonds plummeted, undermining the entire municipal bond market in America, and creating grave financial problems for the state and city of New York, which depended on the bond market for raising money.

Through such magical devices as moral obligation bonds, and similar innovations, Rockefeller managed to print his own species of money for the state. Its debt rose during his administrations from some $1 billion to $13 billion, and most of this new debt was based on nothing more than the Rockefeller-Mitchell concept of moral obligation. Since the banks could only absorb so much of this dubiously-backed debt paper, a day of reckoning was inevitable for the state. The financial forces set in motion by Rockefeller's grand expenditure in the 1960s thus shaped the municipal bond-markets of the 1970s, with New York City the first domino to fall.

In his first effort to secure the Republican nomination for the presidency, in 1964, $12 million of the family money was spent. Nevertheless, Nelson Rockefeller was roundly rejected by the delegates at the Republican convention who enthusiastically endorsed in his stead Barry Goldwater, a senator who strongly identified himself as an ideological conservative and went on to lose the general election by a disastrous proportion of the vote. It thus became evident to Rockefeller that to pursue his presidential ambitions, he had first to resolve a dilemma in image management. While the Republican party regulars insisted on a candidate with an image of a staunch ideological conservative, the independent voters necessary for a Republican victory (since the Republicans were then a minority party) could only be won over by projecting a liberal image. The solution he found was an issue that conveyed a tough conservative image to the law and order elements in the Republican party, but

Laurance S., entrepreneur.   **Nelson A., politician.**

which would not at the same time offend the more moderate elements in the party; it was the suppression of drug addicts.

By proposing measures more draconian than any proposed by Senator Goldwater or his most hardline followers, and thereby hardening his image into that of a conservative, Rockefeller presumed that such a programme would be accepted by even the most liberal of his following, since as he subsequently explained "truly every poll of public concern documents that the number one, growing concern of the American people is crime and drugs – coupled with an all-pervasive fear for the safety of their person and property".

It was this well researched "all pervasive fear" that Rockefeller set out to exploit brilliantly. The crusade against addicts reached its zenith in 1973 when Rockefeller declared that a "reign of terror" existed with "whole neighbourhoods . . . as effectively destroyed by addicts as by an invading army". He pressed through the legislature laws which by-passed both the discretion of the court and the prosecutors by making it mandatory that anyone convicted of selling (or possessing more than $\frac{1}{8}$ ounce of) heroin, amphetamines, LSD, or other specified drugs would be imprisoned for life without the possibility of parole. Even 16-year-old offenders hitherto protected by the youthful offenders law would receive automatic life sentences. Thousand-dollar bounties would be paid for information about these drugs. In another legal innovation the new law laid down life imprisonment (without parole) for the novel crime of *ingesting* a hard drug (including amphetamines or LSD) 48 hours or less before committing any number of proscribed crimes including 'criminal mischief', 'sodomy', 'burglary', 'assault' and 'arson'. This law made it possible to round up any and all undesirable users in society, and put them in prisons for the balance of their life, since they had only to be convicted of a minor crime after ingesting drugs to which they were addicted.

183

As Rockefeller anticipated, the passage of such laws, which the legislature passed with only a few modifications, created a furore in the Press which quickly enhanced Rockefeller's reputation among the hardline element of the Republican party without losing very much support anywhere else – as few people in America were concerned with the fate of drug addicts. To his more moderate supporters, Rockefeller justified the law by explaining, as he did in his senate testimony, "about 135,000 [addicts] were robbing, mugging, murdering day in and day out for their money to fix their habit, and it was costing the people of New York up to $5 billion". Rockefeller had obviously learned in his long experience in psychological warfare that numbers could be effectively employed in political rhetoric, even if they had no basis in fact, if they only sounded enormous and authoritative enough. In this case, if Rockefeller's alleged army of addicts maintained the "day in, day out" schedule they would have to commit something in the order of 49,275,000 robbings, muggings and murders a year, which would mean that the average resident of New York would be robbed, mugged and murdered approximately seven times a year.

In fact, there were about 110,000 such crimes reported in New York City in 1973, or only 1/445 of the crimes that Rockefeller claimed were being committed solely by addicts. Even here, as Rockefeller was well aware, virtually all analyses showed that addicts were responsible for only a minute fraction of the violent crimes he was attributing to them in his constant rhetoric. A report by the Hudson Institute, commissioned by Rockefeller, entitled *Economics of Heroin Distribution*, concluded that less than two per cent of addicts financed their habits by either robbery or muggings (they also concluded that there was only a fraction of the number of hardened addicts that Rockefeller claimed).

To be sure, police usually do blame addicts for a great deal of petty larceny. The Rockefeller estimate that this amounted to $5 billion – which is almost one third of all retail sales in New York City – was, however, pure hyperbole. In 1972, in all, less than $250 million worth of property was reported stolen in the city. After studying the problem, the Hudson Institute reported back to Governor Rockefeller pessimistically "No matter how we generate estimates of total value of property stolen in New York City, we cannot find any way of getting these estimates above $500 million per year." (This was in 1970 when the rate of reported crimes was actually higher than in 1972). The governor, a former co-ordinator of information, found it unnecessary to accept such a statistical defeat – he simply arrived at a figure of $5 billion and then attributed it all to a swarm of addicts, which, in the vocabulary of fear he was articulating, took the place of mediaeval vampires.

Rockefeller correctly foresaw that a programme for imprisoning some 25,000 addicts (that was the number he was giving in those days) without necessarily a trial or a crime being committed would bait his liberal opponents, especially Frank D. O'Connor, the former prosecutor for New York. When in the heat of the campaign, O'Connor did in fact criticise Rockefeller's rehabilitation programme as "an election year stunt" and "medically unsound", Rockefeller had his issue. In speech after speech he asserted as he did at a rally in Brooklyn on November 1, 1966, "Frank O'Connor's election would mean that narcotics addicts would continue to be free to roam the streets – to mug, snatch purses, to steal, even to murder, or to spread the deadly infection that afflicts them possibly to your own son or daughter. Half the crime in New York City is committed by narcotics addicts. My programme – the programme Frank O'Connor pledges to scrap – will get addicts off the streets for up to three years of treatment, aftercare and rehabilitation . . ." With masterful vampire imagery, Rockefeller exploited and agitated the popular fear that the population of New York would be decimated by a horde of addicts, infecting the innocent children of the electorate, if his opponent was elected. Rockefeller easily won the election because, as a Democratic leader explained on CBS Television: "[O'Connor] underestimated the fear of the people about rampant crime . . . parents are scared that their kids might get hooked and turn into addicts themselves; the people want the addicts off the streets and they don't care how you get them off."

Through the agency of the generalised fear of drugs, Rockefeller was able not only to win elections but to project in the popular imagination a new nationwide crisis which he alone, among the nation's politicians, had the experience to solve. A newly created commission which supposedly supervised the involuntary rehabilitation of addicts, but which had on its staff many more public relations specialists than medical doctors and psychiatrists, systematically developed through its own nationally circulated newspapers (*Attack*), newsletters and contacts with the media, the highly dramatised image of heroin addicts as drug slaves, who were ineluctably compelled to steal and ravage by their incurable habit. The size of the addict population in New York proved infinitely flexible. When it was necessary to demonstrate the need for more police measures or judges, Rockefeller expanded 185

Nelson Aldrich Rockefeller: backed by the family billions, he rose as far as Vice-President.

the number of putative addicts from 25,000 (1966) to 150,000 (1972) to 200,000 (1973). For other audiences, especially when Rockefeller wanted to show the efficacy of his programme, the army of addicts was conveniently contracted to under 100,000.

By December 1971 the army of addicts in New York had been hyped up to such proportions that Rockefeller could seriously write in the *New York Law Journal*, "How can we defeat drug abuse before it destroys America? I believe the answer lies in summoning the total commitment America has always demonstrated in times of national crisis . . . Drug addiction represents a threat akin to war in its capacity to kill, enslave, and imperil the nation's future; akin to cancer in spreading of deadly disease among us and equal to any other challenge we face in deserving all the brainpower, manpower and resources necessary to overcome it." He then asked rhetorically, "Are the sons and daughters of a generation that survived the great depression and rebuilt a prosperous nation, that defeated Nazism and Fascism and preserved the free world, to be vanquished by a powder, needles and pills?" Indeed, Rockefeller played the politics of fear so adroitly that President Nixon borrowed much of his rhetoric, images and statistical hyperbole on drugs and crime, when launching his own national heroin crusade.

Although Rockefeller's draconian rhetoric and drug laws had no notable effect on either drug addiction or crime rate in New York, they helped him to achieve the national prominence and acceptance by the hardline elements of the Republican party that he needed if he was to stand for the presidency when Nixon's final term of office was due to expire in 1976. In December 1973, in what members of his staff foresaw as the beginning of the presidential campaign, Rockefeller resigned as governor (thus promoting his faithful lieutenant, Malcolm Wilson, to the governorship) and announced that he was going to spend his full time directing the Commission on Critical Choices, which he had set up with family and foundation money several months earlier. *Ostensibly*, this Commission was designed to "seek a clearer sense of national purpose" but, as did the earlier Rockefeller panels, the well financed organisation also served as a vehicle for gathering together the most important shapers of public opinion in America and, with their assistance, determining issues of public policy they should support. To articulate possible positions the Commission also paid various academics fees ranging from five to thirty thousand dollars. Every word they wrote was scrutinised by the former governor's Press secretary, Hugh Morrow, to gauge the political impact it might, if published, have on Rockefeller's political profile. Deletions and changes were ordered whenever there was even a remote possibility of a scholarly finding conflicting with Rockefeller's public (or planned) stance, as one expert on the administration of justice found out when his thoughtful essay on the crime issue was edited for political purposes.

The political plan for 1976, however, had to be radically altered after the collapse of the Watergate coverup made it apparent that President Nixon would not finish his term of office. Nixon's vice president, Spiro Agnew, was forced from office because of another scandal involving bribe-taking, and he was replaced by Gerald Ford, the popular Republican congressman from Michigan. When Nixon resigned in August 1974, and Ford became president, with another term available to him in 1976, Rockefeller's chances for the presidential nominations were effectively ended. He therefore eagerly accepted Ford's offer to appoint him vice president.

Congressional hearings revealed that, as governor, Rockefeller had made payments of various kinds to key officials, and it emerged too that family funds had been 'laundered' to finance surreptitiously the publication of a book unfavourable to one of his political opponents, but even so the image of Rockefeller and his family as philanthropists had been so successfully established that the payments were dismissed as excessive philanthropy, and the book as an error of judgement. Rockefeller was thus confirmed by both houses as vice president by a wide margin, in which capacity he rapidly managed to become a political strategist for his president.

As America was approaching its bicentennial anniversary then, the Rockefeller brothers had ascended to great political, as well as economic power. Nelson was a heartbeat away from the presidency; David was the undisputed leader of the financial community, able through the agency of the Chase Manhattan bank to determine the fate of a municipality, such as New York City, dependent on the bond market; John D. III was not only financing a good part of the bicentennial celebrations themselves, but through his cultural organisations, held great sway in the intellectual world; Laurance had greatly expanded the family fortune, and this in its turn, virtually beyond assessment, was still intact and administered from the fastnesses of Rockefeller Center.

In a world inimical to the private fortune, the Rockefeller achievement is no mean one. Few American families have adapted so well to the stringencies of their age and managed at the same time to expand rather than weaken their sphere of influence.

186

David Rockefeller (centre), Chairman of the 'family firm', the Chase Manhattan Bank.

INDEX

Page references in bold type refer to illustrations.
Titles of books, plays, magazines, newspapers, ships, paintings (if specifically named) are listed in italic.

ACKNOWLEDGEMENTS

Acknowledgement and thanks for their kind permission to reproduce the following photographs are due to: Associated Press for photographs on pages 116–17 and 119; Camera Press on page 163; Cornell Capa, page 184; Culver Pictures, pages 28, 30, 31, 34–5, 36, 38–9, 41, 44, 45, 46, 47, 48, 50, 51, 53, 99, 111, 112, 132, 133, 140–1, 142, 144, 155, 167, 169, 175 and 178; Detroit Institute of Arts, pages 62–3; Ede Rothaus, pages 14–15, 91, 102–3, 104–5, 108, 114–15, 120, 121, 123, 125, 126, 128–9, 130–1, 134–5, 136–7, 138–9, 143, 144–5, 146, 170–1, 172, 176–7, 180 and 181; Franklin D. Roosevelt Library, pages 147, 148–9, 150–1, 152–3, 154, 156–7, 158–9, 160, 161, 163 and 166–7; Henry Ford Museum, pages 59, 60–1, 64, 65, 66, 67, 68–9, 70, 71, 72, 73, 77, 86, and 88–9; Historical Society of Pennsylvania, page 14; International Museum of Photography, pages 56, 57, 78–9, 94, 95, 98–9; Lady Castle Stuart, page 107; Magnum Photographic Library, page 187; Massachusetts Historical Society, pages 12–13, 16–17, 18–19, 21, 23, and 24; Museum of Society of Photography, page 162; New York Historical Society, page 30; New York Library, page 118; New York State Historical Association, pages 8–9; Paul Popper Photos, pages 164–5; Snowdon, pages 75 and 101; State Historical Society of Colorado, pages 92, 93, 96–7, and 174; United Press International Photography, page 183; Vanderbilt Museum, pages 30, 43, and 52; Wayne State University, pages 80–1, 82–3, and 84–5; White House Historical Collection, page 14; Widener Library, Harvard University, for the photograph on the end papers; Yale University Art Gallery, pages 10–11. The Publishers wish to thank the following for permission to use copyright material in the text: Council of the Humanities on pages 142, 154, 160 and 162 and Curtis Brown on page 136. Every effort has been made to trace the owners of copyright material; if the publisher has in any instance failed to do so, he would be grateful to be informed of the fact in order that the appropriate adjustment may be made in subsequent editions of the book.